Graceful Beginnings

Short and Easy for Anyone New to the Bible

Songs of the Heart
That Light My Way

Psalms that nourish your love for God

MELANIE NEWTON

JOYFUL
WALK
BIBLE
STUDIES

Songs of the Heart That Light My Way: Psalms that nourish your love for God

Published by Joyful Walk Press. Flower Mound, TX.

ISBN: 979-8-9926517-3-7

We extend our heartfelt thanks to the women who served as editors for this study—Connie Crowley, Diana Bravenec, Julie Cox, Julie Hassell, Karen Smith, Lala Cano, Lisa Mosley, Marlo Brazeal, and Kim Newton.

For questions about the use of this study guide or for bulk orders, please email us at melanienewton.com/contact.

Cover picture (Stoica Adrian Image-St Valentine's Day greeting card with candle and hearts.png) from canva.com, used by permission.

Melanie Newton is the author of "Graceful Beginnings" books for anyone new to the Bible and "Joyful Walk Bible Studies" for established Christians. Her mission is to help women learn to study the Bible for themselves and to grow their Bible-teaching skills to lead others.

Joyful Walk Bible Studies are grace-based studies for women of all ages. Each study guide follows the inductive method of Bible study (observation, interpretation, application) in a warm and inviting format.

We pray that you will find *Songs of the Heart That Light My Way* to be a resource that God will use to strengthen you in your faith walk with Him.

Christ-Focused • Grace-Based • Bible-Rich

JOYFUL WALK PRESS
Flower Mound, TX

MELANIE NEWTON

Melanie Newton is a Louisiana girl who made the choice to follow Jesus while attending LSU. She and her husband Ron married and moved to Texas for him to attend Dallas Theological Seminary. They stayed in Texas where Ron led a wilderness camping ministry for troubled youth for many years. Ron now helps corporations with their challenging employees and is the author of the top-rated business book, *No Jerks on the Job*.

Melanie jumped into raising three Texas-born children and serving in ministry to women at her church. Through the years, the Lord has given her opportunity to do Bible teaching and to write grace-based Bible studies for women that are now available from her website (melanienewton.com) and on Bible.org. *Graceful Beginnings* books are for anyone new to the Bible. *Joyful Walk Bible Studies* are for maturing Christians.

Melanie Newton loves to help women learn how to study the Bible for themselves. She also helps women grow their Bible-teaching skills to lead others—all with the goal of getting to know Jesus more along the way. Her heart's desire is to encourage you to have a joyful relationship with Jesus Christ so you are willing to share that experience with others around you.

Jesus took hold of me in 1972, and I've been on this great adventure ever since. My life is a gift of God, full of blessings in the midst of difficult challenges. The more I've learned and experienced God's absolutely amazing grace, the more I've discovered my faith walk to be a joyful one. I'm still living that joyful walk every day...

Melanie

OTHER BIBLE STUDIES BY MELANIE NEWTON

Download our catalogue and get resources for your spiritual growth at melanienewton.com.

Graceful Beginnings Series books for anyone new to the Bible:

A Fresh Start (basics for new Christians)
Painting the Portrait of Jesus (the Gospel of John)
The God You Can Know (the character of God)
Grace Overflowing (an overview of Paul's 13 letters)
The Walk from Fear to Faith (7 Old Testament women)
Satisfied by His Love (women who knew Jesus)
Seek the Treasure (study of Ephesians)
Pathways to a Joyful Walk (6 pathways to a life filled with joy)
Songs of the Heart That Light My Way (selected Psalms)

Joyful Walk Bible Studies for growing Christians:

Adorn Yourself with Godliness (1 Timothy and Titus)
Everyday Women, Ever Faithful God (Old Testament women)
Connecting Faith to Sight (Genesis 1-11)
Graceful Living (the essentials for a grace-based Christian life)
Graceful Living Today (a devotional journal for a joyful life)
Healthy Living (Colossians and Philemon)
Heartbreak to Hope (the Gospel of Mark)
Identity: (Ezra thru Malachi)
Knowing Jesus, Knowing Joy (Philippians)
Live Out His Love (New Testament women)
Perspective (1and 2 Thessalonians)
Profiles of Perseverance (Old Testament men)
Radical Acts (Acts)
Reboot, Renew, Rejoice (1 and 2 Chronicles)
The God-Dependent Woman (2 Corinthians)
To Be Found Faithful (2 Timothy)

Resources for leading others:

Be a Christ-Focused Small Group Leader
Leap into Lifestyle Disciplemaking
Painting the Picture of Jesus (the "I Am's" of Jesus for children)
Teaching Children the God They Can Know (the character of God)

Contents

Introduction

GRACEFUL BEGINNINGS

The *Graceful Beginnings Series* of Bible studies are specifically designed for anyone new to the Bible—whether you are a new Christian or you just feel insecure about understanding the Bible. The lessons are basic, introducing you as an inexperienced Christian to your God and His way of approaching life in simple terms that can be easily understood.

Just as a newborn baby needs to know the love and trustworthiness of her parents, the new Christian needs to know and experience the love and trustworthiness of her God. *A Fresh Start* is the first book in the series, laying a good foundation of truth for you to grasp and apply to your life. The other books in the series can be done in any order.

SOME BIBLE BASICS

Throughout these lessons, you will use a Bible to answer questions as you discover treasure about your life with Christ. The Bible is one book containing a collection of 66 books combined together for our benefit. It is divided into two main parts: the Old Testament and the New Testament.

The Old Testament tells the story of the beginning of the world and God's promises to humanity given through the nation of Israel. It tells how the people of Israel obeyed and disobeyed God over many, many years. All the stories and messages in the Old Testament lead up to Jesus Christ's coming to the earth.

The New Testament tells the story of Jesus Christ, the early Christians, and God's promises to all those who believe in Jesus. You can think of the Old Testament as 'before Christ' and the New Testament as 'after Christ'.

Each book of the Bible is divided into chapters and verses within those chapters to make it easier to study. Bible references include the book name, chapter number, and verse number(s). For example, Ephesians 2:8 refers to the New Testament book of Ephesians, the 2nd chapter, and verse 8 within that 2nd chapter. Printed Bibles have a Table of Contents in the front to help you locate books by page number. Bible apps also have a contents list by book and chapter.

TRANSLATION CHOICES

The Bible verses highlighted at the beginning of each lesson in this study are from the New International Version® (NIV®) unless otherwise indicated. You can use any version of the Bible to answer the questions, but using a translation that is easier to read and understand will help you gain confidence in understanding what you are reading. We recommend these versions: NIV, CSB, NLT, NET, ESV. You can easily find these translations in the "YouVersion App" or on www.biblegateway.com.

This study capitalizes certain pronouns referring to God, Jesus, and the Holy Spirit—He, Him, His, Himself—just to make the reading of the study information less confusing. Some Bible translations likewise capitalize those pronouns referring to God; others do not. It is simply a matter of preference, not a requirement.

If you have an older translation of the Bible such as King James or early New American Standard, you will run across the pronouns Thou, Thy, and Thee referring to God in the Psalms or in recorded prayers. These are holdovers from Old English *(thy = you singular)* that became incorporated into Middle English (time of Shakespeare) when used in formal, legal speech. Thus, the pronouns were incorporated into the King James Bible translated during that time (1611 AD). There is no magical or spiritual aura about these words. Most modern translations have elected to use the pronouns we use in our English language today. Yet, many people still love hearing those old pronouns in reference to God.

OLD TESTAMENT SUMMARY

About 1700 years after God created everything, He sent judgment on a rebellious race through a worldwide Flood. He later separated the nations with different languages and scattered them from Babel. Abraham, Isaac, and Jacob were the patriarchs (ancestors) of the Hebrew people. Sold into slavery, Joseph became a powerful foreign leader. The Israelites developed into a great nation for ~400 years in Egypt, until their deliverance from bondage. Then Moses took the people across the Red Sea and taught them God's Law at Mt. Sinai. Joshua led the Israelites into the Promised Land after a 40-year trek in the wilderness because of unbelief.

During the transition toward monarchy, there were deliverer-rulers called "judges," the last of whom was Samuel. The first three Hebrew kings—Saul, David, and Solomon—each ruled 40 years. Under

Rehoboam, the Hebrew nation divided into northern and southern kingdoms, respectively called Israel and Judah. Prophets warned against worshipping the foreign god Baal. After the reign of 19 wicked kings in the north, Assyria conquered and scattered the northern kingdom. In the south, 20 kings ruled for ~350 years, until Babylon took the people into captivity for 70 years. Zerubbabel, Ezra, and Nehemiah led the Jews back into Jerusalem over a 100-year period. More than 400 'silent years' spanned the gap between Malachi (end of the Old Testament) and Matthew (beginning of the New Testament).

The 39 books in the Old Testament are divided into 4 main categories:

> THE LAW (Genesis through Deuteronomy)—Israel's start as God's chosen people; God giving His Laws (called the Law of Moses) to the people making them distinct from the other nations.

> HISTORY (Joshua through Esther)—narratives that reveal what happened from the time the people entered the Promised Land right after Moses died until 400 years before Christ was born.

> POETRY & WISDOM (Job through Song of Solomon)—take place at the same time as the history books but are set apart because they are written as poems and have a lot of wise teaching in them.

> PROPHETS (Isaiah through Malachi)—concurrent with the books of history and, except for Lamentations, reflect the name of the prophet through whom God spoke to the nation of Israel.

OLD TESTAMENT TIMELINE

This book covers poems, prayers, and songs written by several Old Testament people over a span of 1,000 years. To help with historical context, here is a simple Old Testament timeline.

Historical Period	Years BC	Psalm Authors
The Patriarchs	2100 - 1800	
Israel in Egypt / the Exodus	1800 - 1450	Moses
Conquest of land / Judges	1450 - 1050	Hannah
United Kingdom	1050 – 900	David, Solomon, Asaph
Divided Kingdom	900 – 586	Sons of Korah
Exile and Post-Exile	586 - 400	

ELEMENTS OF EACH LESSON

This short and easy study covers selected psalms from the Old Testament.

1. Each lesson begins with a BIBLE VERSE that relates to the focus of the lesson and a prayer. Prayer is just talking to God as conversation with someone who loves you dearly. The BEGINNING PRAYER simply asks Jesus to teach you through the lesson.

2. PSALMS INSIGHTS: Several of the lessons have a short section at the beginning with information related to studying the Old Testament and the Psalms in particular.

3. This is followed by a simple study of the psalm being covered in the lesson. Read the Bible verses and answer the associated questions. This study uses the NIV translation. We recommend you use that or these other translations (CSB, NLT, NET, ESV). See "Translation Choices" (page 2) for online sources of these.

4. In the "SONGS OF THE HEART" section at the end of the study questions, you will be encouraged to dwell more on what you learned in the lesson that nourishes your love for God today.

5. DEEPER DISCOVERIES (OPTIONAL): These are additional reading of specific psalms that are similar in focus to the one highlighted by the lesson.

SMALL GROUP DISCUSSION

While you can work through these lessons as a personal study, this topic is perfect to use for small groups. Share the following suggested guidelines with the group members to maximize your discussion group experience.

➢ Set aside some time each week to do the study questions so that you will get to know God better.

➢ Consistently attend whether your lesson is done or not. You will learn from the discussion.

➢ Respect each other's insights. Listen thoughtfully. Share your own insights, but do not dominate the discussion.

➢ Celebrate unity in Christ by avoiding controversial subjects such as politics, divisive issues and denominational differences.

➢ Maintain confidentiality of whatever is shared within the group.

Enjoy your small group discussion and learn from one another. As you reflect on parts of your story and share that with your group members, you will have a greater connection with each other. And, you'll have more reason to praise our loving God as you see and hear how He has been faithful to each of you through the years.

Suggested Leader Guide for Group Discussion:

Discussing the lesson (apart from the "DEEPER DISCOVERIES" readings) should take about an hour, making this an easy study to fit into a busy workday schedule.

1. Pray for the Lord Jesus to teach you what He wants you to know through the lesson.

2. Work through the LESSON together, reading the Bible verses and discussing the questions. Predetermine which of the explanatory paragraphs you will read as a group. Others you might point out the highlights and move to the next one.

3. Read the "SONGS OF THE HEART" section and share responses to any application questions.

4. If you have time, ask what they learned from the DEEPER DISCOVERIES readings.

5. Pray for the group members using the prayer prompts at the end of the lesson.

6. Remind each person to do the next lesson before the group meets again.

SONGS OF THE HEART THAT LIGHT MY WAY

The title of this book, *Songs of the Heart That Light My Way,* reflects this well-known verse from Psalm 119:

> *Your word is a lamp for my feet, a light on my path. (Psalm 119:105)*

God reveals Himself through His Word, the Bible. We get to know who He is and how much He loves us. That encourages us to trust Him and follow His leading in our lives. Through what He teaches us in His Word and trusting Him enough to follow that, we learn to live our lives His way rather than the world's way. In a real sense, His Word lights our way.

Psalms are songs of the heart. They are poems, prayers, and praises directed to God from the heart of a believer. As lyric poetry, they are filled with metaphors, hyperboles, and other creative expressions, especially of emotion.

Every emotion experienced by human beings is represented in the psalms: fear, anger, depression, joy, resentment, confidence, and gratitude. You will see the psalm writers expressing their gut-wrenching emotions to God then coming away with a renewed heart because of the truth affirmed to them while in God's presence.

As a Christian, you can likewise go right to the presence of God and pour out your heart to Him in all circumstances. He can renew your mind with truth to guide your behavior and emotions. And He will give you a renewed heart—one that loves and trusts Him more. In this study, we will learn that the psalms light our way to loving God and trusting Him more.

I have chosen several of my favorite psalms for us to study together. Each one of them has nourished my love for my God and filled my heart with joy as I walk with Him through each day. May they do the same for you. It is going to be a great journey. And I am so glad to be walking alongside you!

Melanie Newton

Psalm 8: My God Is My Creator

LORD, our Lord, how majestic is your name in all the earth! (Psalm 8:9)

Pray: Lord Jesus, please teach me through your Word.

PSALMS INSIGHTS—THE ABCS OF PSALMS

Like any book you read, it always helps to know a bit about the **author**, the **background** setting for the story (i.e., past, present, future), and where the book fits into a series (that's the **context**). The same is true of Bible books.

Authors

The book of Psalms is one of the great treasure chests of the Bible. It is a collection of 150 poems, prayers, and praises (each called a 'psalm') written by Jews in the time before Christ. Because most were also sung to the accompaniment of various instruments, this collection became the hymnal of the Jewish people.

David wrote nearly half of them (73) before and after he was king. His son Solomon wrote 2. Asaph (David's choir leader) and his descendants wrote 12. The sons of Korah (a family of Levitical musicians) wrote 9, and Moses wrote 1. The rest are mostly anonymous. All have been preserved by God for us to have in our Bibles.

Some songs that can be called psalms are not included in this book. Two examples are Deborah's song (Judges 5) and Hannah's prayer (1 Samuel 2). We will cover Hannah's 'psalm' in Lesson 8.

Background

Like the other books of the Old Testament (except for Genesis and Job), the psalms represent the Jewish people living under the Law of Moses (commonly called 'the Law') in the land of Israel. It is important to keep that background in mind when studying them.

Some of the psalms give information about the author, place, or purpose for their writing. We will see one example of this in Psalm 34 (Lesson

3). More than 50 of them have the subtitle "For the choir director" or "For the director of music," suggesting that psalm was used for congregational singing. Most of the psalms, however, do not have any subtitles, so we don't know the author or the background of that individual psalm as in Psalm 107 (Lesson 6).

God's covenant relationship with Israel and its people is the foundation for the history, promises, and hopes expressed in the psalms.

Context

In our Bibles, the book of Psalms is found in the middle of the Old Testament. It covers about 1000 years of history from the Exodus (Psalm 90 written by Moses) to Psalm 137 (written after the return from exile in Babylon). You can refer to the simple Old Testament timeline (page 3) to see the different parts of Israel's history.

Before 400 BC, the Jews collected the individual psalms and compiled them into five 'books'. Each 'book' ends with a dedicated praise to God. Psalm 150 is a grand finale for the whole collection. Chronological Bible reading plans try to match individual psalms with a specific era of Israel's history, helping to give context to those psalms.

Someone who is new to the Bible could easily get overwhelmed looking at the book of Psalms with its 150 individual chapters. Relax. It isn't necessary to read or study all of them at one time. It isn't necessary to read them in order. The psalms are randomly collected even though the Jews put them in 'books'. It's okay to pick and choose which ones you would like to read or study. I've chosen just a few of my favorites to highlight in this study guide.

You can use any Bible translation for this study. I use the NIV primarily, so the questions reflect that.

WHY STUDY THE PSALMS?

Did you know that the book of Psalms is quoted more often in the New Testament than any other Old Testament book? That adds to its importance in the context of the Bible and reasons why we should study it. The psalms provide insight into how the people of ancient Israel related to the God they knew and trusted.

Unlike the prose of the gospel narratives or doctrinal teaching in Paul's letters, the psalms are lyric poetry These poems are addressed primarily to God and filled with metaphors, hyperboles, and other lyrical expressions, especially of emotion. Every emotion humans experience is represented in the psalms: fear, anger, depression, joy, resentment, confidence, and gratitude. You'll see the psalm writers expressing their gut-wrenching emotions to God. They then come away with a renewed heart and nourished love for God because of the truth affirmed to them while in God's presence.

As a Christian, you can likewise go right to the presence of God and pour out your heart to Him in all circumstances. He can renew your mind with truth to guide your behavior and emotions. And He will give you a renewed heart—one that loves and trusts Him more. In this study, we will learn that the psalms light our way to loving God and trusting Him more.

> Your word is a lamp for my feet, a light on my path. (Psalm 119:105)

As we read and study these psalms together, we will seek first to understand what the authors understood in their time and place. What were they thinking and feeling and experiencing? We will use New Testament teachings to add application to our lives today as needed.

Reading the book of Psalms will nourish your love for God and your trust in Him for everyday life.

What grabbed your attention from the information above?

Ready to dig into these wonderful poems and prayers that are a gift from God to us? We begin by reading the whole psalm to get the big picture before we study the verses more closely.

PSALM 8

David wrote this psalm. We know that David was a shepherd boy who slew the giant Goliath (1 Samuel 17) and grew up to be a great king of Israel. We can read about his life in 1 and 2 Samuel, 1 Kings, and 1 Chronicles. We also know that Jesus Christ descended from David's house, and there are fifty-nine references to David in the New Testament.

David is the only person in the Bible whose scriptural epitaph reads "a man after God's own heart" (1 Samuel 13:14; Acts 13:22). God said this about him while he was just a teen faithfully doing work related to family life—before he did anything great. We can glean insight into what David thought and felt by reading many of the 73 psalms he wrote, such as this one we will be studying. David's name means 'beloved', and we see evidence of this in his writing.

Psalm 8 is one of the 50 psalms that marvel at God's creation. As you read, consider the times when you likewise marvel at God's creation.

Read Psalm 8 silently then read it aloud.

This song was for the director of music, meaning it was likely intended for congregational singing. Historians think "Gittith" is a musical term.

In general, what is David feeling?

What grabbed your attention from your reading?

To whom is this psalm addressed (verse 1)?

David knew God by the personal name *Yahweh* (Hebrew, pronounced YAH-weh). In our English translations, it is usually written as LORD in all capital letters. It is the name by which God wanted to be known and worshiped by Israel. *Yahweh* means, "I am." This name expressed His character as **constant, dependable, and faithful**.

Following LORD, David used the phrase "our Lord" (not in all capital letters). The Hebrew word he used there refers to "master, king." The LORD is the sovereign king over all His creation, including people David acknowledges God as his king and master over his heart and life. David's humility recognizes God's authority over him.

Jesus applied God's name "I am" to Himself (John 4:26; 8:58), thus declaring Himself to be God. The ever-faithful, promise-keeping God of the Old Testament is embodied in the Lord Jesus Christ of the New

Testament and forever. We still have a personal God who is the king and master of our hearts and lives.

David begins and ends this short psalm with the same declaration (verses 1 and 9). Write it in the space below.

God's name refers to His revealed character and who He is—His reputation. Various translations use the words 'majestic', 'magnificent', and 'excellent' to describe God's name.

So what did David think about God?

What can be seen in the heavens (verse 1)?

Because God's name and glory are evident all over the earth, who gives praise to Him (verse 2)?

Their praises silence whom?

God's glory is the visible expression of His greatness and worth, certainly seen in the heavens. The praises of babies and children silence "the foe and the avenger (NIV)." The foe represents God's enemies—those in rebellion against Him. The avenger is anyone who strikes back against His followers in malicious revenge (Psalm 44:16).

Read Matthew 21:12-16 (first book in the New Testament).

This is a fulfillment of Psalm 8:2. Jesus is in Jerusalem at the Temple 'cleaning house' and healing people (verses 12-14)

From verses 15-16 ...

- Who were the enemies?

- Who was praising Jesus and how?

Have you noticed how small children easily love Jesus? It's as though they come out of the womb ready to love the God who made them. Yet, older more sophisticated adults often deny Him. Sadly, they are the ones who often teach the children to give up their love for God.

Focus on Psalm 8:3-4.

David said that God covered the heavens with His glory and majesty. In the Bible, people used the term *heaven* to describe three different 'realms'—the sky, the universe, and a spiritual heaven. God's glory and majesty are seen in all three. David focused on the universe "heavens."

What does David see in the universe (verse 3)?

What are your thoughts when you view and consider the vastness of the heavens above you?

When looking at the vastness of God's realm in the heavens, what amazed David in verse 4?

The heavens are the work of God's "fingers." Our God is separate from His creation and is in authority over it. His splendor exceeds that of the heavens. As frail human beings, we tend to feel insignificant and unimportant as we glimpse the vastness and splendor of God's creation. Yet the amazing truth is that *we matter more to God than words can describe.* You and I are highly significant to God!

Focus on Psalm 8:5-8.

The word translated "heavenly beings (ESV)" or "angels (NIV)" often refers to God Himself. Your translation might say "God." All are true.

God has done what for us humans (verse 5)?

What responsibility has God given to us (verses 6-8)?

God created humans to be lower than Himself but higher than the animal kingdom. David marveled that God gave the dominion of the earth to humans which also confirms their dignity in God's sight.

Read Genesis 1:26-27.

"Let us" and "our" refer to the triune God—Father, Son, and Spirit. Our God is one God in 3 persons. The New Testament especially reveals this mysterious truth about our God. God the Father sent God the Son to earth to live as a human, die for our sins on the cross, and rise from the dead. Then, God the Spirit came to permanently live inside all believers. He is the one who helps us to understood the Bible as we study it.

What is unique about the creation of human beings?

So how important are we as human beings to God?

Created in His image

The 'image of God' refers to His character, not a physical image. It includes what God has enabled humans to do plus who we are. That means we have a spirit that enables us to relate to God. The human spirit was created to be a container for God's Spirit.

Read 2 Corinthians 3:18

As the Spirit works in us, we are being what (3:18)?

Read 2 Corinthians 4:6-7.

What does God put in us as frail "jars of clay" (4:6-7)?

God makes His light shine in our hearts as we get to know and love Him more. We can know our God more through knowing His Son, Jesus Christ. Christ lives in us through the Spirit making us the walking, talking representatives of the living God. Others see Jesus through us.

We know that sin has tarnished the image of God in us. But it has not erased it. The fact that we are created in the image of God could, and should, have a tremendous impact on how we view ourselves and our place in the world.

Unfortunately, our significance and importance to God are not usually the messages that we receive in our daily lives. Consider how secular teaching that we are evolved animals affects your understanding of your importance to God and your place in His world.

Those who are opposed to God as Creator would rather choose to have evolved from an amoeba than accepting the Bible's teaching of humans being created in God's image. So they suppress the truth about God (Romans 1:18-20).

What do you learn from Psalm 8 to counteract that false teaching?

Science belongs to God. No believer needs to be afraid of it. True science will also provide information that agrees with what is revealed by God in the Bible about His work of creation and more. Go to icr.org to get credible scientific answers to your questions about God's creation.

Ruling His creation under His authority

God called His creation "very good" and placed all living creatures under the rule of Adam and Eve at the beginning. He did not withdraw that responsibility after they sinned. Under His sovereignty as King, God still delegates to humans the responsibility of managing what is His—all creatures and plants. We have not done it well because of our sinfulness. Yet, we are to continually work together to do this for Him.

The writer of Hebrews quotes Psalm 8:4-8 in Hebrews 2:5-8. He applies the ultimate ruling over all creation to Christ. Christ is recognized as the Son of Man (a name He applied to Himself) who has dominion over the earth now and is to have dominion over the future redeemed creation. We are joint heirs with Him in this ruling over our planet. The creation is groaning because of sin (Romans 8:19-22). One day, everything will be fixed. We will still have a part in the managing of God's creation. That day will fulfill Psalm 8:5-8.

Our God is a majestic sovereign who has remarkably entrusted His magnificent creation to frail humans who are also the capstone of His creation. Amazing! We are to willingly submit to His authority and live in dependence upon Him as we fulfill our purpose of ruling over His creation. We are not to live as puffed-up, self-reliant humans who think we are the lord of our lives.

I love that my God is my Creator. Do you recognize Him as your Creator?

SONGS OF THE HEART

God reveals Himself through His Word, the Bible. We get to know who He is and how much He loves us. That encourages us to trust Him and follow His leading in our lives. Through what He teaches us in His Word and trusting Him enough to follow that, we learn to live our lives His way rather than the world's way. His Word lights our way to loving God and trusting Him more, as the psalm writers did with their 'songs of the heart'.

What do you learn about God from this psalm?

How does this psalm nourish your love for God?

Choose one verse from this psalm to write in the space below. Ask your Lord to teach you through this verse.

Most of the psalms were intended to be sung showing the important role of music in our spiritual lives and especially in our worship. Music is a gift from God. His people through the centuries have composed lyrics and music that are likewise to be sung in community worship. So in this study, we will end each lesson with one of our modern 'psalms' that reflect something in the psalm we studied. You can listen to them on YouTube by searching the song title.

When I gaze into the night sky, And see the work of Your fingers. The moon and stars suspended in space.
But what is man that You are mindful of him?
You have given man a crown of glory and honor.
And have made him a little lower than the angels.
You have put him in charge of all creation;
The beasts of the field, the birds of the air, the fish of the sea.
But what is man, oh, what is man That You are mindful of him?
O Lord, our God, the majesty and glory of Your name
Transcends the earth and fills the heavens.
O Lord, our God little children praise Him perfectly.
And so would we, and so would we.
Alleluia, Alleluia. The majesty and glory of Your name!
("The Majesty and Glory of Your Name," Linda Lee Johnson
and Tom Fettk)

Pray: Take some time this week to gaze at the moon and stars, a sunrise or a sunset, while reading Psalm 8 aloud. Realize just how important you are to God, and spend your time thanking Him for who He is and for creating you in His image and giving you purpose in this life to serve Him. Ask Him to help you depend on Him more than on yourself and be His representative to others as you live each day.

DEEPER DISCOVERIES (OPTIONAL):

Spend a few minutes reading and reflecting on the following psalms that also speak of the sovereignty and majesty of God in His creation.

Read Psalm 104. Reflect on what you read.

Read Psalm 148. Reflect on what you read.

Psalm 19: My God Is My Rock

May these words of my mouth and this meditation of my heart be pleasing in your sight, LORD, my Rock and my Redeemer. (Psalm 19:14)

Pray: Lord Jesus, please teach me through your Word.

PSALMS INSIGHTS

Hebrew poetry

Hebrew poetry, including all the psalms, is unlike western poetry. It is not based on rhyme or meter as in "the rain in Spain falls mainly on the plain." Instead, Hebrew poetry is based on parallelism and rhythm. So, the beauty of the rhythm and imagery survives translation into other languages better than anything dependent on rhyme or meter.

➤ **Parallelism**: The writer states an idea in the first phrase of a couplet (two lines). This idea is either repeated or contrasted in the second line.

➤ **Rhythm**: The accent is on important words, often action verbs written in successive sentences.

You will see both types of parallelism in Psalm 19 as well as recognizable rhythm.

Types of psalms

Various scholars have tried to classify the psalms in order to understand them better. Some psalms were obviously a spontaneous outpouring of a heart filled with praise and/or pain. These are readily noticeable as you read them. Other psalms were more carefully crafted by the author, often following a specific structure or written for congregations to use in public worship (leader reading and congregation responding).

The following list contains the most common types of psalms. Those we will be studying are in italics.

➤ **Praise:** These describe specific characteristics of God worthy of praise or answers to prayer that generate gratitude in the heart of the psalmist. *Psalm 8; Psalm 34; Psalm 139; Hannah's song*

➤ **Wisdom:** These psalms describe God's way of approaching life and how following His way leads to a blessed life. *Psalm 19; Psalm 34; Psalm 139*

➤ **Lament or Petition:** Something in the psalmist's life that is causing pain or sorrow triggers the petition to God to do something about it. *Psalm 73*

➤ **Trust.** These psalms recognize God as provider and protector and worthy of the faithful believer's trust in Him. *Psalm 103; Psalm 107*

➤ **Acrostic:** Each verse or stanza begins with the consecutive letters of the Hebrew alphabet. *Psalm 34*

PSALM 19

Like Psalm 8 (Lesson 1), David wrote this psalm and designated it for the director of music. Music was a big part of Hebrew worship of God. From the earliest days of Israel's existence, men and women played musical instruments and sang songs to praise God and thank Him for being good to them. As king of Israel, David worked diligently to organize and enhance the public worship gatherings. He assembled gifted musicians for the worship band (men and women singers plus those who played harps, lyres, and cymbals). He divided them into smaller groups who would serve for two weeks at a time as praise and worship leaders. Psalm 19 would certainly be a beautiful song for that purpose.

As you study, you will see why this psalm is called a wisdom psalm.

Read Psalm 19 silently then read it aloud.

In general, what is the writer feeling?

What grabbed your attention from your reading?

Revelation of God in the Skies

Focus on Psalm 19:1-6.

Notice the repeat parallelism especially in verses 1-3—heavens declare / sky displays; day after day / night after night; and no speech / no sound.

> *Like Psalm 8, the writer views God's creation in the skies above him. What do the heavens declare (verses 1-2)?*

> *This soundless communication extends how far (verse 3-4 first part)?*

David then focuses on one created object he sees—the sun. The heavens are like a tent that God has made for the sun (verse 4).

> *Under God's direction, what does the sun do (verse 6)?*

> *Is any area on the earth excluded from knowing about God through His creation of the universe?*

The heavens declare the glory of God and the work of His hands. Everything we see in the sky and beyond is a non-verbal testimony to God's existence. Even the sun, which pagan religions worshiped as a god, is only a work of God's mighty hand and does His continual bidding over all the earth. It is celebrated each day like a bridegroom at his marriage or an athlete rejoicing at running a race. No part of our planet is unreached. Everyone can understand it regardless of what language they speak. The testimony is that God exists, is more powerful than anything else, and worth knowing. We can see and feel the message being proclaimed.

That truth is confirmed in Paul's letter to the Romans in the New Testament.

Read Romans 1:18-20.

> *What can be clearly seen and known about God from His creation (verse 20)?*

> *God makes this plainly known to people so they are what (end of verse 20)?*

Every human can see and know God's eternal power and divine nature from what He has made. We can know that God exists from what we see in the expanse of space. God's creative handiwork is evident to all humans everywhere on our planet who are looking at it. This is called **general revelation**.

> When you lie on your back and gaze at the stars, you realize it is the closest thing to infinity that you will see before you die. (Dr. Stanley Toussaint, "God's Revelation and Our Response")

Revelation of God in the Scriptures

Focus on Psalm 19:7-10.

God also speaks to us through the Scriptures—Old and New Testaments. This is called **specific revelation**. Through His written Word, God reveals His plan to bless all humankind.

In this psalm, David used different terms with similar meanings for God's instructions to humans regarding His way of living life. This example of poetic rhythm celebrates the life-nurturing effects of the Lord's revealed Word to us.

The words below are from the NIV. Your translation might use different words like those in parentheses. There are two descriptions in each verse.

How is God's Word described and what does it do for us?

VERSE 7:

- Law (instruction)—

- Statutes (testimony / rules / decrees)—

VERSE 8:

- Precepts (statues / commandments)—

- Commands (commandment)—

VERSE 9:

- Fear (reverence)—

- Decrees (judgments / ordinances / rules)—

God's Word reveals His will for us to know. It is perfect, trustworthy, right, radiant, pure, and firm. Knowing and obeying God's Word brings rewards. It refreshes us and makes us wise. It gives us joyful hearts and bright eyes reflecting God's light in us and showing us the way to live. One Bible teacher called it 'God's vitamin box.' The Creator of the universe has given us this very personal book—our Bible. That is amazing!

Our Response to God's Revelation

Focus on Psalm 19:10-14.

Gold was the most expensive substance of David's day. Honey was considered the sweetest.

> *Why are God's statutes and decrees more precious than gold and sweeter than honey (verse 11)?*

We have already seen some of the rewards in verses 7-9. David then considers other rewards. Knowing the Scriptures can help us stay true to our God by warning us of that which does not please God.

> *The Scriptures can help you discern what (verse 12)?*

> *The Scriptures can also help you do what (verse 13)?*

God's Word can bring to light behaviors displeasing to God that are otherwise unrecognized. Those are called unintentional sins ("hidden faults"). Then, we can confess our guilt, recognize God's forgiveness, and ask Him to help us change our ways. God's Word gives us boundaries so that we can live to please God.

Notice the poetic contrast in verse 13. Willful (deliberate) sins are intentional and represent open rebellion against God. The Law made sacrificial provision for unintentional sins. But for intentional sins, the person threw themselves on the mercy of God and asked Him to forgive them so their relationship with God would be restored.

David asked God to bring any willful, deliberate sins to his notice so they would not rule over him or dominate him. In contrast to willful sinning, the opposite lifestyle would be to ask God to keep you away from such deliberate sin. Then, you will be blameless in His sight and free from the baggage of sin. That is a reward for obedience to God's revelation.

Your response to the Word of God opens your heart to God. That is expressed in the last verse of this psalm.

After seeing God's revelation in creation and His revealed Word, what does the writer desire in his heart (verse 14)?

Do you desire the words of your mouth and the meditation (thoughts) of your heart to be pleasing to God? If not, why not?

Emotions are a big part of our everyday lives and experience, sometimes dictating how we think and act. We can be pretty fickle when it comes to submission. We don't like having to submit in the areas God desires for us to submit, but we often gladly submit to our emotions and let them rule us.

As Christians, we don't need to submit to our emotions. Instead , we can fill our minds with God's truth. Learning how to think right will influence our behavior as well as our emotions. It doesn't mean we won't ever have negative emotions such as fear, anger, worry, or depression. The psalms we are studying show how real those emotions are to even faithful believers in God.

The words in this wisdom psalm can teach us what to do with those emotions. We are to listen to God's Word and apply it to our lives so that we can live to please our God.

Consider the wisdom from this long-time Bible teacher:

> God would rather I have understanding of two verses that I obey immediately than twenty verses that I don't. Obedience is the key to discernment. It's not 'capture and remember'; it's 'hear and obey'. (Chip Ingram)

Isn't that true? What is your response to God's Word?

You can consider the Bible to be beneath us and reject it. You can put yourself on an equal standing with the Bible, accepting some parts and rejecting others. Or you can put yourself under the Bible and say to God, "Teach me, Lord, for Your servant is listening."

When we approach God with a humble and teachable heart, He will lead us through His Word and help us to apply it in our lives. My trust is to be in God leading me, not in me leading myself. He does that through His Word. That is why we start each lesson with this prayer, "Lord Jesus, please teach me through your Word."

Who is God to David (end of verse 14)?

What do you think of when you hear the word 'rock'? As a geologist, I think of the thick layers of solid rock that build the mountains—strong and unmovable. To me, mountains are majestic like God's name and reputation as we learned in Psalm 8. God is our Rock.

God is also our Redeemer. A redeemer is one who delivers you from something not good for you. Sin is not good for you, especially willful sins. The consequences of sin can destroy your life and the lives of those around you. Responding to God's instructions about how to live life sets us free from the control of sin (verse 13). Jesus did that for us through His finished work on the cross. As believers in Christ, we are redeemed from the bondage to sin that we once had. We will see this again in Psalm 107.

God has made Himself known to us in many ways—in nature, in the Bible, and supremely in the Lord Jesus who is the image of the invisible God (Colossians 1:15). Such revelation should make us bow in humble adoration and willing obedience before the One who created us.

I love thinking about God as my Rock. Is He your rock?

SONGS OF THE HEART

What do you learn about God from this psalm?

How does this psalm nourish your love for God?

Choose one verse from this psalm to write in the space below. Ask your Lord to teach you through this verse.

Isaac Watts was a prolific hymnwriter of the 18th century. The following hymn is one of his most famous. It is one of my favorites as well.

> I sing the mighty pow'r of God, that made the mountains rise,
> That spread the flowing seas abroad, and built the lofty skies.
> I sing the wisdom that ordained the sun to rule the day;
> The moon shines full at His command, and all the stars obey.
> I sing the goodness of the Lord, who filled the earth with food,
> Who formed the creatures through the Word, and then
> pronounced them good.

Lord, how Thy wonders are displayed, where'er I turn my eye,
If I survey the ground I tread, or gaze upon the sky.
There's not a plant or flow'r below, but makes Thy glories
known,
And clouds arise, and tempests blow, by order from Thy
throne;
While all that borrows life from Thee is ever in Thy care;
And everywhere that we can be, Thou, God, are present there.

("Sing the Mighty Power of God," Isaac Watts, 1715)

Pray: Thank God for His revelation to you in nature and in the Scriptures. Ask Him to teach you through His Word and help you to obey it so that the words in your heart and mouth are pleasing to Him. Thank Him for being your Rock and your Redeemer.

DEEPER DISCOVERIES (OPTIONAL):

Spend a few minutes reading and reflecting on the following psalms that are also wisdom psalms.

Read Psalm 37. Reflect on what you read.

Read Psalm 40. Reflect on what you read.

Psalm 34: My God Is My Refuge

Taste and see that the Lord is good; blessed is the one who takes refuge in him. (Psalm 34:8)

Pray: Lord Jesus, please teach me through your Word.

PSALMS INSIGHTS—UNDERSTANDING THE OLD TESTAMENT

The psalms were composed by people living under the Law of Moses (commonly called 'the Law'). It is important to keep that context in mind when studying them. Some words and concepts used by Old Testament writers such as the psalmists have different meanings to Christians today. Being aware of the differences will help you understand the truth revealed about God and His way of doing life with Him.

In the Old Testament:

> ➤ '**Save**' and '**Salvation**' are generally used to mean *deliverance* from earthly trouble or danger rather than spiritual or eternal salvation as we are accustomed to using those words. You will see an example of this in Psalm 34:17-18.

> ➤ '**Judge**' usually refers to God or God's representative acting as a hero or knight in shining armor to defend **justice** and the plight of the poor and defenseless. It does not usually refer to a courtroom setting.

> ➤ '**The Holy Spirit**' came upon certain individuals *temporarily* to empower them for special service (such as artisans, prophets, or kings). The Spirit then left when that service was completed.

> ➤ '**Forgiveness of sins**' under the law was accomplished through *atonement*, which means a 'covering' for sin (the animal sacrifices). A gracious God offered forgiveness to those who trusted in His lovingkindness, but it was at best *temporary* and *up-to-date*. The sacrifices in the law did not provide someone forgiveness for tomorrow's sins.

As you read the Old Testament books, read first to obtain accurate understanding of what their authors meant. Then, use New Testament teachings to apply truth about God to your everyday life in Jesus Christ. We will do that in this study.

PSALM 34

This psalm was one of several written by David at a specific time in his life. After being anointed as a teenager to be the next king of Israel, he spent most of the next 13 years or so 'on the run' from the current king Saul. God had rejected Saul as king, and Saul was not happy about it. He tried numerous times to kill David. The psalms David wrote during that time are like a journal revealing what David was thinking and feeling during his years of flight from Saul.

David tried hiding in the Philistine city of Gath, pretending to be insane so as not to appear a threat to Abimelech the king. But he was driven away from Gath. It was a time of great turmoil in David's life. The story is recorded in 1 Samuel chapter 21. David wrote Psalm 34 during that time. The truths expressed in it are for us to know and apply as well.

Though not recognizable in English translations, Psalm 34 is an acrostic poem. Each verse begins with the successive letters of the Hebrew alphabet. That means David carefully crafted it. Other acrostic psalms are 9, 10, 25, 37, 111, 112, 119, and 145.

Regarding content, Psalm 34 is another wisdom psalm. This is especially seen in verses 8-22.

Read Psalm 34 silently then read it aloud.

In general, what is the writer feeling?

What grabbed your attention from your reading?

Focus on Psalm 34:1-7.

What is the writer doing in verses 1-2?

David is inviting others to do what in verse 3?

David sought the Lord in his difficult situation. How does God respond (verses 4 and 6)?

What truth does David know and declare about God based on his own experience in ... ?

- Verse 5—

- Verse 7—

To glorify the Lord means to magnify Him, to see Him bigger. Don't keep Him in a little box in your imagination. Make others know how important He is. David invited people to join him in praising God verbally and publicly so others can hear and rejoice with us. That is a way to glorify the Lord.

Those who look to God are radiant (verse 5). The underlying Hebrew word means to sparkle, to stream forth light. We saw in Psalm 19:8 that trusting in God's Word gives joy to the heart and radiant light to the eyes. And believers who are trusting God reflect His glory that He puts inside of us through His Spirit. We learned that from Psalm 8. Haven't you seen Christians who have joy in their eyes? Regardless of what is going on around us, we need to remember He is with us and in us. There is no shame in trusting Him.

David's praise on this occasion was especially for being delivered from his fearful situation (verses 4, 6, and 7). The "angel of the Lord" is perhaps the LORD Himself, as used in many other Old Testament situations. With eyes of faith, David saw Him surrounding and protecting His people—those who trust in Him. Isn't this a beautiful word picture? We'll see this same idea in Psalm 139.

In 1 Samuel 22:1-5, we can see how God answered David's prayer for deliverance. God helped him to escape to a cave 'hideout'. David's family came to join him there as well as about 400 men who became his army and some of his closest friends. God also sent the prophet Gad to give David direction about where to go next for his protection. God rescued him from the immediate danger, though David remained on the run for several more years.

Focus on Psalm 34:8-14.

David follows up with more truth that he knows about God. Notice the poetic rhythm of action verbs in verses 8, 9, 11, 13, and 14.

In verse 8, what action does David invite you to take?

In verse 9, what does David invite you to do?

Those who fear (reverence) and seek Him lack what (verses 9-10)?

In verse 11, what action does David invite you to take?

David's wisdom appeals to whom (verse 12)?

What wise action does David invite you to take in ... ?

- Verse 13—

- Verse 14—

How would taking the actions in verses 8, 9, 11, 13, and 14 lead to enjoyment of life (verse 12)?

David invited people to taste and see that our God is good. To taste means to personally try something. You can taste and see God's goodness as you trust Him with your time of distress or challenge. Doing that strengthens your faith.

David wants to instruct others from what he has learned himself about God's goodness. God's deliverance of David was only one example of His goodness. Our God is good all the time—even in the tough times, in different ways to each of us, and in what He allows or doesn't allow into our lives.

Mighty lions may lack food and grow weak, but those who trust in God will lack nothing (verse 9), lack no good thing (verse 10). That is huge! When we have God with us, we lack nothing we need at the time. The reference in verse 12 to "many good days" may not refer to years of life but to the quality of joyful life knowing God is on our side and with us.

God's method of teaching us is this: prepare by instruction, learn by experience. When you prepare yourself through instruction from God's Word and apply that as you live each day, you learn how to trust God more. Then, you can really see that He is good in whatever choice He makes to answer your prayers for deliverance.

Focus on Psalm 34:15-20.

What truth about God does David know (verse 15)?

What is also true about God (verse 16)?

What do verses 4, 6, 15, and 17 have in common?

The Lord not only rescues those in trouble or danger, but who else receives His attention (verse 18)?

The righteous person may have what (verse 19)?

The 'eyes' and 'ears' of the Lord are attentive to the righteous. The righteous are those who have faith in Him. When they cry out, God hears and acts on their behalf. Doesn't that make you feel loved?

And the Lord is close to those who are brokenhearted and feel crushed in spirit by the way others treat them. Don't you love that? You don't have to be in some major trouble for God to care. He sees your heart and cares about you when you hurt.

But those who continue to rebel against Him do not get that treatment. God is always against evil and will do whatever He needs to do to rid His creation of the pollution from sin.

Notice that God doesn't prevent the righteous from having troubles or being in dangerous situations requiring His rescue. Yet, verses 19 and 20 are a general expectation. "All his bones" (verse 20) refers to the inner skeleton that gives your body support.

God allows certain things to happen by His choice and goodness, but His choice will not destroy our inner strength because God supports us through it all.

Focus on Psalm 34:21-22.

David knows that God enacts His justice on the wicked (verse 21). Sometimes He uses the consequences of their own actions. That would include a nation's justice system.

This is like a fork in the road. You can choose your own evil ways, or you can choose to follow God's ways and trust His goodness in whatever He chooses to do for you.

What is the promise to those who serve God (verse 22)?

Notice that the phrase "take refuge in Him" appears at the beginning of this section (verse 8) and then again at the end (verse 22)—like bookends. David's personal experience in verses 1-7 is followed by his appeal to others to trust God as he does (verses 8-22).

We all have frightening or humiliating experiences that are begging for deliverance. Our God responds to us when we cry out to Him. He promises to anyone who trusts in Him that they will be rescued in some way from their trouble. They will lack no good thing that they need. They will never be condemned like those who do evil. Their faces will be radiant and never covered with shame. Isn't that the better choice? The best choice!

A BIBLICAL PERSPECTIVE OF TROUBLE

The New Testament gives us more insight into how we should view trouble in our lives.

Read 2 Corinthians 4:7-9, 16-18.

As we experience troubles in this world, we may be hard pressed on every side, but not crushed. We may be perplexed about what is happening, but we will not be in despair. When we are persecuted, we are not abandoned by God. We may be struck down but never destroyed.

> *How should we view hard things happening to us (verse 17)?*

That is an amazing perspective—our "light and momentary troubles." There is more to this life than what we experience now. Yet the promise in Psalm 34:20 and in 2 Corinthians 4:16 is that God will keep renewing our inner strength so that we can endure them without losing heart.

One of the challenges to us when we have troubling situations that others have caused is the temptation to want revenge.

Read Romans 12:17-21.

> *What are we not to do?*

- Verse 17—

- Verse 19—

What are we to trust God to do (verse 19)?

While waiting for God to avenge us, we are to do what to our enemy (verses 20-21)?

Do not take revenge but let God be your avenger. You know how hard this is to do. When you place your trouble in God's hand and trust His choice in what to do about it, you can be confident that He will be your avenger in His time. Let Him do it!

Consider this perspective when facing your troubles:

> Stop telling God how big your problems are and start telling your problems how big your God is. (Wayne Braudrick, *Pause* sermon on Psalm 46, 1/5/25)

I love that God is my Refuge. Is He your Refuge?

SONGS OF THE HEART

What do you learn about God from this psalm?

How does this psalm nourish your love for God?

Choose one verse from this psalm to write in the space below. Ask your Lord to teach you through this verse.

When we are afraid, we can know that God is our refuge and rescuer. This is one of my favorite modern songs confirming this truth.

> You hear me when I call, You are my morning song
> Though darkness fills the night, It cannot hide the light
> Whom shall I fear?
> You crush the enemy, Underneath my feet
> You are my sword and shield, Though troubles linger still
> Whom shall I fear?
> My strength is in your name, For you alone can save
> You will deliver me, Yours is the victory
> Whom shall I fear?
> I know who goes before me, I know who stands behind
> The God of angel armies Is always by my side
> The one who reigns forever He is a friend of mine
> The God of angel armies Is always by my side
> And nothing formed against me shall stand
> You hold the whole world in your hands
> I'm holding on to your promises You are faithful
> You are faithful You are faithful
> I know who goes before me, I know who stands behind
> The God of angel armies Is always by my side
> The one who reigns forever He is a friend of mine
> The God of angel armies Is always by my side
> ("Whom Shall I Fear," Chris Tomlin, Ed Cash, Scott Cash)

> **Pray:** *Turn over your troubles to God, and believe that He is attentive to you as His child. Trust Him to rescue you, strengthen you, and provide whatever you need so that you lack no good thing.*

DEEPER DISCOVERIES (OPTIONAL):

Spend a few minutes reading and reflecting on the following psalms that speak of God's protection and deliverance from difficult situations.

Read Psalm 56. David wrote this one during the same time period. Reflect on what you read.

Read Psalm 91. Reflect on what you read.

Psalm 73: My God Is Enough

Yet I am always with you; you hold me by my right hand. You guide me with your counsel, and afterward you will take me into glory. (Psalm 73:23-24)

Pray: Lord Jesus, please teach me through your Word.

PSALMS INSIGHTS—SALVATION AND ETERNAL LIFE

People were saved by faith in the Old Testament.

In the Old Testament, God's grace accepted any person who came to Him by faith. For example, Abraham believed God and that belief made him righteous in God's eyes (Genesis 15:6). Being declared righteous qualified him for eternal life. Like Abraham, those who believed God also received eternal life by their faith alone. That is consistent with what the New Testament teaches (Galatians 3:9,14).

God's method of **managing** His people, however, was different. So **how** one's faith was expressed and lived out differed as well. The Tabernacle and the Temple represented the presence of God dwelling among His chosen people, Israel. There, the priests represented the people to God. Sacrificial offerings were the prime way for the people to publicly express worship, repentance for sin, and thanksgiving.

God wanted the worshiper's **heart** first. Where one's **heart** was right, sacrifices could be acceptable to God as an expression of inner faith. When the heart was not right, the sacrifices were not accepted. While we no longer express worship to God through animal sacrifices, He still desires the **hearts** of His people above all else.

People are saved by faith in the New Testament.

When Jesus Christ died on the cross, He brought to a close the age of the Old Covenant—the Law of Moses. He simultaneously inaugurated the New Covenant in which we now live. Salvation is obtained by faith in Christ and His finished work on the cross. Every believer in Christ receives forgiveness for all sin—past, present, and future. Salvation is also secure and never taken away.

As we saw in Psalm 34, God continues to deliver His people from some things but not from all dangers. He uses some challenges to teach us to rely on Him more than on ourselves (2 Corinthians 1:9). New Testament believers since the time of Christ have a permanent indwelling of the Holy Spirit who gives us eternal life and His daily empowering presence.

PSALM 73

This is one of a collection of psalms attributed to Asaph and his descendants. The first Asaph lived during the time of King David and was the leader of one of the choirs that led worship in Jerusalem—either in front of the tent that held the Ark of the Covenant or in front of the Temple once it was built. Asaph's descendants continued to lead singing as the Jews gathered for worship at the Temple.

Read Psalm 73 silently then read it aloud.

In general, what is the writer feeling?

What grabbed your attention from your reading?

This is a lament psalm. A lament is a passionate expression of grief, sorrow, or something you feel is wrong. You likely saw this as you read. It is also a wisdom psalm because it helps the reader seek trusting God above whatever the disappointment is (verses 23-26 especially). It is a story of ups and downs in life and how to think rightly about them.

THE QUESTION—WHY DO THE WICKED PROSPER?

Focus on Psalm 73:1-3.

Verse 1 is actually the writer's conclusion at the end of his very painful struggle to find the truth as recorded in this psalm.

What does the writer believe to be true about God (verse 1)?

In his faith walk, what had almost happened to him (verse 2)?

Why (verse 3)?

The writer began by affirming God's goodness to His people, especially those who are "pure in heart." Pure of heart refers to a single-minded commitment to God, following Him faithfully. You see references to the heart throughout this psalm—verses 1, 7, 13, 21, and 26.

Then, he confessed that he nearly stumbled in his faith as he compared his life with the great material prosperity of the wicked—the ones who were rebelling against God in their hearts and lives. They are mocking God openly and still doing great!

Focus on Psalm 73:4-12.

These verses describe the psalmist's view of the wicked.

What does the writer observe about the wicked in ... ?

- Their comfort (verses 4-5)—

- Their arrogance (verses 6-7)—

- Their words (verses 8-9)—

- Their influence (verse 10)—

- Their thinking (verse 11)—

- Their prosperity (verse12)—

Have you let envy of the carefree life of wicked people affect you? What were you thinking and feeling?

The psalmist saw that the wicked are proud, violent, unrestrained, and maliciously threaten others. They also influence others to do the same and act as if God does not know or even care how they live. So they continue to prosper. They are acting like spiritual terrorists in the community. How could God ignore that?!

Focus on Psalm 73:13-17.

In light of his observations about the wicked, what is the writer feeling?

- Verse 13—

- Verse 14—

If he had spoken his resentment publicly, he would have done what (verse 15)?

Trying to understand why the wicked prosper did what to him (verse 16)?

The psalmist is asking the age-old question, "Why do the wicked prosper?" His basic response to what he sees around him is this, "What do I get for following God?" It is easy to look around and see wicked people prospering while you are not. Doesn't God see?

To the people of Israel, God had promised general blessings on the faithful and curses on the wicked (Deuteronomy 28). The psalmist wasn't seeing this around him and in his own life. He is expressing doubt. Doubt is a mind struggling to believe but wanting to believe. That is different from the unbelief of the wicked. Unbelief is an unwillingness to believe in God and surrender to Him.

The writer is troubled by his own suffering. Instead of prospering, he sees only problems that plague him daily—perhaps chronic illness, poverty, etc. He is perplexed about God's lack of punishment of the wicked. He isn't saying that he wants to be like the wicked. He is feeling that there should be a reward for being good.

Have you ever felt that there should be a recognizable reward for being good, but you are not seeing it? How did that affect you?

Asaph wisely chose not to declare his feelings publicly and thus cause mischief to others' faith. He would have misled them because he was not considering all the facts. We likewise must be careful with whom we express our doubts. Talk it out with God and other strong Christians but not to new or young Christians who are still trying to break away from the world's influence. Then, give your doubt to God and choose to trust Him.

Where does the psalmist go in his struggle with his feelings (verse 17)?

What does the writer remember when he went into the sanctuary of God (end of verse 17)?

For individuals in the Old Testament, God dwelt among His people in different specific ways, one of which was in His 'sanctuary.' At first, it was the Tabernacle, a moveable tent used while Israel was in the wilderness and the first few hundred years Israel was in their land. David moved the tent to Jerusalem shortly after he conquered the town and made it Israel's capital. Then, King Solomon built the Temple which became the sanctuary of God. This was a permanent dwelling place for God's presence (1 Kings 8:27-30).

Asaph went to God's sanctuary. If he was a priest, he could go inside the actual structure. If not a priest, he could stand in front of it in the court of the Israelites. Either way, he was in God's presence. There, he began to view life according to God's perspective. He remembers that there is another life after this one. And God gets the final say.

Today, God's presence dwells in His people by His Holy Spirit, and we who know Him are ourselves His temple (see 2 Corinthians 6:16). As believers in Jesus Christ, we can confidently approach God's presence, referred to in Hebrews 4:16 as His 'throne of grace' with confidence.

We enter God's presence today through His Word and through prayer. There, we can also get His guidance on any part of life that puzzles us.

THE ANSWER — KNOWING GOD IS FAR BETTER!

Focus on Psalm 73:18-20 and 27.

At first the psalmist saw himself on slippery and uncertain ground (verses 2-3), but now he sees the situation differently. It is the wicked who are on the slippery slope (verse 18).

Why are the wicked on a slippery slope (verses 18-19)?

What is their destiny (verse 27)?

God gives freedom to the wicked to live as they choose. But their way of life is like walking on ice. It can and will result in an eventual fall. Like a dream that vanishes upon wakening (verse 20), the lives of the wicked will vanish one day. They will be cast down, destroyed, swept away, and despised. We saw in Psalm 34:21 that their own evil will eventually be their downfall. At the end of this life, they will stand before God. His justice will condemn them. I heard someone say that this is the only heaven they will ever know. That is very sad, isn't it?

Focus on Psalm 73:21-26.

As the psalmist looks back on his time of doubt (verse 21), how does he describe himself (verse 22)?

He was dense and full of bitterness—senseless and ignorant of God's guidance. He was wallowing in self-pity. He couldn't think straight. Holding onto anger and bitterness at the unfairness in this world only hurts us and blinds us to the truth. We lose perspective. We cease to trust God.

The psalmist remembers his relationship with God and what it means to know Him. The words he used next are so personal. Knowing that God is just as available to you as He was to the writer of Psalm 73, fill out the following questions from a *personal* perspective.

You are always with whom (verse 23)?

What is God doing (verse 23)?

He guides you with what (verse 24)?

What happens after this life (verse 24)?

What can compare to having God in your life (verse 25)?

Even when your body wears out, what is promised to you (verse 26)?

God is always with you, guiding you with His counsel from His Word—the Bible. Your flesh and heart may fail, but God is your strength now and will continue to be your strength. God is your portion—the source of happiness and blessing. God will hold your hand all the way through this life and past this life into the glorious next one. You have a future with God in heaven. It is the presence of God that makes heaven a glorious place. One day, Jesus will come for you to take you there (John 14:3).

The psalmist is willing to go without the great material advantages of the wicked because he had an enduring relationship with God. He knows that he has the best inheritance imaginable and decides not to seek any possession or comfort outside of God. He is content with all that the Lord is and provides. That was **enough** for him.

As we learned in Psalm 34:9-10, we lack no good thing when we have God. That is what Asaph declared in verse 25. "Whom have I in heaven but you? And earth has nothing I desire besides you." Jesus' disciples recognized the same thing and asked a similar question, "Lord, to whom shall we go? You have the words of eternal life. We have come to believe and to know that you are the Holy One of God (John 6:68-69)."

You can persevere through anything in this life if you believe that when you have God, you need nothing else. He loves you dearly. And like a good father, He grabs your hand to give you comfort and strength. Picture yourself sitting with Jesus, holding out your hand for Father God to take hold and whisper in your ear, "Don't be afraid, I am helping you."

> *What difference does (or would) having this perspective in your relationship with God make in your life?*

Focus on Psalm 73:28.

> *After considering what he has with God, what is the writer's conclusion (verse 28 first part)?*

> *What does he plan to do (verse 28 second part)?*

In Psalm 73:15, the psalmist refrained from speaking to others because he knew what he would say would not be right and good. As he comes to his conclusion in verse 28, he now has something to say. Being with God is enough.

Asaph once envied the wicked but now pities them. He has far more than they will ever have. They are missing out on the greatest blessing of all because they refuse to believe in the God who is real and wants a relationship with them.

What do you get for following God? **You get HIM!** What more do you really need? He is your refuge against the wicked and against your own self-pity. He is enough.

LAMENTING VERSUS WHINING

The pattern of a lament psalm is to tell God: "I'm in trouble. You're not listening. The bad guys are winning. But I will trust in You." Crying out in anger and frustration to God is biblical. Genuine lamenting comes from a heart that admits you are deserving of nothing. You have a heart of humility before God. Lamenting is honest-to-God dialogue.

Whining, on the other hand, presupposes that you are entitled to something and usually contains selfish motives. "I want what I want when I want it—now! And do it my way!" Whining is not pleasing to God. Just read the story of the Israelites' journey in the wilderness to see that (the book of Numbers especially)!

Paul also confirmed that for us.

> ***Do everything without grumbling or arguing***, *so that you may become blameless and pure, "children of God without fault in a warped and crooked generation." (Philippians 2:14-15)*

Lamenting takes whatever problems you see and carries them into the presence of God, giving Him opportunity to teach you something from it. Usually, He teaches you something about yourself or teaches you how to want His will more than your own. In the midst of your questions and complaints, stop and bring them to the Lord. Let Him lead you in your thinking about whatever your complaint is. Psalm 73 shows you how to do that.

I have learned through the years of many challenges that my God is enough. Is He enough for you?

SONGS OF THE HEART

What do you learn about God from this psalm?

What do you learn from this psalm about handling doubts, envy, or bitterness that are 'slippery places' causing you to stumble in your faith walk?

Choose one verse from this psalm to write in the space below. Ask God to teach you through this verse.

This song has been one of my favorites for several years. It reminds me that regardless of the good and bad around me, my God is enough.

> Blessed Be Your Name, In the land that is plentiful
> Where Your streams of abundance flow, Blessed be Your name
> Blessed Be Your name, When I'm found in the desert place
> Though I walk through the wilderness, Blessed Be Your name
> Blessed be Your name, When the sun's shining down on me
> When the world's 'all as it should be,' Blessed be Your name
> Blessed be Your name, On the road marked with suffering
> Though there's pain in the offering, Blessed be Your name
> You give and take away, You give and take away
> My heart will choose to say, Lord, blessed be Your name
> Every blessing You pour out I'll turn back to praise
> When the darkness closes in, Lord Still I will say
> Blessed be the name of the Lord, Blessed be Your name
> Blessed be the name of the Lord, Blessed be Your glorious name
> ("Blessed Be Your Name," Matt Redman, Beth Redman)

Pray: Tell God whatever is bothering you. Ask Him for His guidance so you can see clearly. Thank Him for His nearness and goodness to you. Ask Him to help you be content with whatever He provides for you.

DEEPER DISCOVERIES (OPTIONAL):

Spend a few minutes reading and reflecting on the following psalms that are laments, especially about what looks to be unfair in this world.

Read Psalm 49. Reflect on what you read.

Read Psalm 77. Reflect on what you read.

Psalm 103: My God Loves Me

Praise the Lord, my soul; all my inmost being, praise his holy name. Praise the Lord, my soul, and forget not all his benefits… (Psalm 103:1-2)

Pray: Lord Jesus, please teach me through your Word.

PSALMS INSIGHTS—SPECIFIC WORDS

It helps to understand the meaning of some words that are frequently used in the book of Psalms.

Bless, Blessed—translates the Hebrew word *barak,* meaning to be happy, in a state of well-being. When used of God ("Bless the Lord"), it means to praise and thank Him as the source of all our blessings. English translations of the psalms use 'bless' or 'praise' interchangeably. You can see this in translation comparisons of Psalm 103:1, 2, 20, 21, and 22.

Meditate—means to read the same thing over and over, think about it, and consider what it says. To meditate does **not** mean making your mind blank or clear and repeating some mystical word or phrase.

Praise the Lord—often translates the Hebrew phrase *Hallelujah.* The last words in the book of Psalms are this jubilant shout: "Let everything that has breath praise the Lord, hallelujah (Psalm 150:6)!" This declaration defines the whole tone and theme of Psalms. Many of the psalms are centered on the importance of praising the majesty of God— who He is and what He does. David consistently used 'bless the Lord' rather than *hallelujah* in Psalm 103.

Lovingkindness—translates the Hebrew word *hesed,* one of the most wonderful Hebrew words to describe God's love for people. It is God's loyal and faithful love that leads Him to be kind and good to those trusting in Him. The psalmists used this word often. It is hard to describe God's *hesed* with one English word, so it is translated various ways— lovingkindness (NKJV), steadfast love (ESV), faithful love (CSB), and simply 'love' (NIV). *Hesed* is used four times in Psalm 103—verses 4, 8, 11, and 17. Think of *hesed* like the word 'grace' in the New Testament in that God's lovingkindness is based on His gift to us not on our merit.

PSALM 103

This is another psalm written by David.

Read Psalm 103 silently then read it aloud.

In general, what is the writer feeling?

What grabbed your attention from your reading?

Because of a lifetime of knowing God and seeing Him at work, David's heart is filled with praise and thanksgiving. Did you notice that there are no requests in this psalm? Someone once said about Psalm 103, "It is perhaps the most perfect song of praise in the Bible." Let's see why.

Focus on Psalm 103:1-5.

Write verse 1 in the space below.

The writer begins and ends his psalm with the same phrase, "Praise the LORD, my soul" (NIV). He is talking to himself as a reminder to thank God as the source of all His blessings. "My soul" refers to one's total being. What starts on the inside should show up on the outside.

What are we to not forget (verse 2)?

Benefits are anything God gives to help us. When is it easy to forget them?

The benefits listed are God's actions on our behalf. What does He do for us ...?

- Verse 3—

- Verse 4—

What else does God do for us (verse 5)?

God satisfies whatever you need with good things (verse 5). That seems like a summary of what is in verses 3 & 4.

What does it mean to be satisfied?

What do you usually do when you feel unsatisfied?

I love what Moses wrote,

> *Satisfy us in the morning with your unfailing love, that we may sing for joy and be glad all our days. (Psalm 90:14)*

Being satisfied starts with His unfailing love (*hesed*) so that we can experience the joy of life every day.

In Psalm 34, we looked at actions we take to get to know God. Here are God's actions toward us, what David calls His 'benefits.' All of those benefits from God are good things that help us—forgiveness, healing, rescue, assurance of love, and compassion. To be 'crowned' means to be surrounded with His love and compassion so that you have a sense of God's favor and protection. And He fills your life with good things that nourish you and renew your strength. Like eagles who remain strong to the end of their lives, God enables us to stay spiritually strong so we can soar and glide above the woes of this world. All of those good things represent His faithful love for us and satisfy our heart needs.

A feeling of dissatisfaction should alert us to the danger of not embracing God's benefits and seeking other things to replace them. Even when God fed Israel to the full so they lacked nothing, some were not satisfied and went after strange gods. Beware of this, dear Christian.

One particular area of life where we might be dissatisfied is the area of physical illness or pain. When David used the phrase "heals all your diseases," is he promising that God's people will never get sick or stay sick? No. God is not bound to heal every disease. But every healing comes from Him. What could that mean?

God has created the human body with a remarkable ability to heal itself through our marvelous immune system. Yet, you've no doubt seen where the same treatment for a disease will work well for one person but not for another. We don't understand why. Doctors can treat the symptoms, but they have no control over the body's response. Healing still comes from God.

Sometimes, our God miraculously heals in unexpected ways. Other times, God chooses to allow us to have chronic bodily ailments so that we will rely on Him more. That makes us strong (see 2 Corinthians 12:9-10). We must trust God's goodness in what He chooses to do when it comes to healing.

David reminds himself and us to not forget all His benefits. God's people are called to remember who He is, what He has done for us, and who we are in His hands. We can often take credit ourselves for our benefits—physical abilities, education, and opportunities—while forgetting that He gave those to us.

This is important for you to know: Remembering is **not passive**. It is an action that requires turning your heart to God to listen to Him and to obey Him. It is loving God with all your heart, soul, and mind. The result is that you live differently from those around you who reject God. Remembering means that you **choose** not to forget.

Focus on Psalm 103:6-12.

David lists more benefits from the Lord in these verses.

> *What does the Lord do (verse 6)?*

Verse 7 refers to everything written in the Old Testament. Paul wrote in Romans 15,

> *For everything that was written in the past was written to teach us, so that through the **endurance** taught in the Scriptures and the **encouragement** they provide **we might have hope**. (Romans 15:4)*

Through those Scriptures, we get to know our God as David did. In Psalm 103:8, David quotes what he learned from Exodus 34:6.

> *Write Psalm 103:8 in the space below.*

God declared these truths about Himself to Moses and the people of Israel early in their relationship with Him. These truths are stated nine more times in the Old Testament and once in the New Testament. This is the God we can know!

Verses 9-12 illustrate the truth of verse 8.

> *How is His compassion shown to us (verse 9)?*

> *How is His grace / mercy shown to us (verse 10)?*

How great is His love for us (verse 11)?

What does His great love lead Him to do for us (verse 12)?

"Sins" and "iniquities" (verse 10) and "transgressions" (verse 12) all refer to the sinful nature and disobedience to God's commands. God removes those as far as the east is from the west. How far is that? It is unmeasurable, never ending. East and west never touch. By His choice, God completely separates us from the guilt of our sins by forgiving them.

Read Ephesians 2:4-5.

Paul also wrote of God's great love.

What does His love motivate Him to do?

Have you done something that you are afraid is beyond forgiveness?

Read Colossians 2:13-14.

What is true about your sins now?

Your sins are gone. Past, present, and future. Nailed to the cross. Once you trust in Jesus Christ, God no longer keeps an accounting of your sins against you (see 2 Corinthians 5:19). Believe it. Live in that truth. God does this because of His great love for you.

The Pharisees and teachers of the law in the gospels viewed God as harsh, loveless, and exacting—only interested in rule-following. That is why Jesus confronted them so often and bluntly. Their view of God was wrong, and it affected their own lives and those they influenced.

Our faith begins with receiving the love of God and understanding it in the Bible. Many Christians do not know about God's love. That is why theology is important because a goofed-up theology is going to keep you from ever loving God. If you think you have to earn your way to heaven, you might be trying really hard. But you are never going to really love God. When we start with how much God loves us, we then see His love for us in His grace to us that forgives all our sins. This God we can know is revealed in the Lord Jesus Christ. Amen!

Focus on Psalm 103:13-18.

From verse 13, God's compassion is also like what?

From verses 14-16, what does God remember about us so that He has compassion on us?

To whom does God extend His faithful love ...?

- Verse 17—

- Verse 18—

For how long does He love us (beginning of verse 17)?

How do you feel as you read these verses? Do you understand how much God loves you?

Did you see the word picture of God as a father? The concept of God as Father was not unknown to the Jews. The psalmist in Psalm 89:26 says to God, *"You are my Father, my God, the Rock my Savior."* When Jesus taught His disciples to pray, "Our Father," they understood. Jesus continually encouraged His followers to pray to Father God whom they could trust.

Our God is a trustworthy Father and is your Father God too. The moment you placed your trust in Jesus Christ for your salvation, you were adopted into God's family as His child.

Read Ephesians 5:1.

What are you called (end of verse)?

God loves the world. But He has a special love for believers in Him. You are His **dearly** loved children! Beloved! He is the perfect Father, the most loving Father, the most dependable Father, and the Father who cares about your every need. Our Father God's love for you is deep, amazing, and everlasting. It never ends!

Even if you didn't have such a good earthly father, God wants you to know that you are dearly loved by your Father God. Dearly loved. Think of the best father in any book, movie, or TV show. Who comes to mind? God is even better than that father. And you can know Him well, love Him wholeheartedly, and gain the confidence to trust Him as your Father God who loves you.

And God's love for us transcends generations and continues to those who love and obey Him in our households. As we learned in Psalms 19 and 34, obedience leads to the reward of a joyful life. Children and grandchildren benefit from the presence of godly parents.

Focus on Psalm 103:19-22.

David has confidence in God's wonderful benefits to him because he knows what about the Lord (verse 19)?

David emphasizes God's sovereignty and the proper response to it. In His role as universal king, God assures order and justice in the world and among His people. Though we cannot fully see this now, we will see it during the millennial kingdom as King Jesus physically reigns over all on our planet.

While waiting, we must remember who God is, His sovereignty, His love, and His grace toward us embodied in Jesus Christ. Through Jesus, God offers us forgiveness, healing, and hope for dire circumstances, and freedom from bondage to anything. He crowns us with assurance of His love and His compassion. When you remember that truth about your God, you are set free to stop focusing on the 'impossible' and focus on **the God who does the impossible**.

Who and what does the writer invite to join him in praising the Lord (verses 20-22)?

What does verse 20 tell us about angels?

"All His works" (verse 22) includes all creation, which joins the human chorus to celebrate the goodness of God. Angels (heavenly hosts) should praise Him while doing His bidding. Animals, plants, and the physical earth are continual reminders of God as creator and point to Him (Psalm 8 and 19).

This psalm teaches us what God is like and how He loves us. We should join the rest of creation by praising Him because of who He is and how He shows His love to us. We are dearly loved!

I love that my God loves me. Do you love that He loves you?

SONGS OF THE HEART

David ended this psalm as he began it—reminding himself to praise the Lord with a thankful heart. Consider your response of gratitude to Him.

What do you learn about God from this psalm?

Choose one verse from this psalm to write in the space below. Ask God to teach you through this verse.

What do you not want to forget of His benefits? Write a psalm of praise to God—remembering what He has done for you in the past, what He is doing now, and what He has promised for your future. Then, read it to the Lord.

I have often heard the following song on the radio. While working on this study, I realized that this modern psalm fits so well with Psalm 103.

> Who am I, that the Lord of all the earth would care to know
> my name? Would care to feel my hurt?
> Who am I, that the bright and morning star would choose to
> light the way for my ever-wandering heart?
> Who am I, that the eyes that see my sin would look on me
> with love, And watch me rise again
> Who am I, that the voice that calmed the sea would call out
> through the rain, And calm the storm in me?
> Not because of who I am but because of what you've done
> Not because of what I've done but because of who you are
> I am a flower quickly fading here today and gone tomorrow
> A wave tossed in the ocean, a vapor in the wind
> Still you hear me when I'm calling
> Lord, you catch me when I'm falling
> And you've told me who I am. I am yours.
>> ("Who Am I?" songwriter Mark Hall)

Pray: *Thank God for loving you so much and satisfying your heart needs with His love and care for you. Ask Him to help you remember His goodness and love whenever you feel unsatisfied.*

DEEPER DISCOVERIES (OPTIONAL):

Spend a few minutes reading and reflecting on the following psalms that speak of God's goodness and love.

Read Psalm 92. Reflect on what you read.

Read Psalm 111. Reflect on what you read.

Psalm 107: My God Is My Redeemer

*Give thanks to the Lord, for he is good; his love endures forever. Let the **redeemed** of the Lord tell their story—those he **redeemed** from the hand of the foe… (Psalm 107:1-2)*

> *Pray: Lord Jesus, please teach me through your Word.*

PSALM 107

This is a psalm of trust as well as one of thanksgiving. Its style is closely related to Psalms 105 and 106, so they may be from the same unknown author.

Read Psalm 107 silently then read it aloud.

The writer wants to motivate the Lord's people to praise Him by reviewing some of His mighty acts, which are evidence of His faithful love *(hesed)*. We looked at this aspect of God's love for us in Psalm 103 (Lesson 5). It is His steadfast, promise-keeping love.

In general, what is the writer feeling?

What grabbed your attention from your reading?

Did you notice the different kinds of people who call out to God and how He responds to their specific needs? All of them like all of us need deliverance from something. God's lovingkindness *(hesed)* motivates Him to do something to help. This psalm is an application of God's unfailing love for us frail and often foolish humans (Psalm 103:14-16).

Some people think this psalm was written after the time of the Jewish exile in Babylon when groups of Jews returned to their land in Israel. You can get that idea from verse 3, "those [God] gathered from the lands, from east and west, from north and south."

Remember that Hebrew poetry has parallelism often seen as contrast or repeated phrases. There is a lot of parallelism in this psalm. Each section follows a similar pattern—the people in trouble, their need, their cry to the Lord, His deliverance, how He met their need, and how they should respond to His lovingkindness to them. The writer used the same phrase describing what those in trouble did.

What did they do (verses 6, 13, 19, and 28)?

What did God do every time?

Remember that 'saved' and 'delivered' in the Old Testament refer to **deliverance** from earthly trouble or danger rather than spiritual or eternal salvation as we are accustomed to using the word **saved**.

The writer likewise repeats what the proper response to God's deliverance should be.

What should the 'delivered' do (verses 8, 15, 21, and 31)?

Focus on Psalm 107:1-3.

Write verse 1 in the space below.

God's lovingkindness and goodness are reasons we should give Him our thanks and praise.

What are we then to do and why (verse 2)?

If you are a Christian, tell others how good our God is. He is good!

The word 'redeemed' means released from bondage to something or someone. In Psalm 107, the people needing help are "redeemed from the hand of the foe" (verse 2). We will look at what the foe (trouble) is for each of the groups described.

Those Who Are Wandering

Focus on Psalm 107:4-9.

The writer of this psalm describes those who are wandering, seeking something to satisfy their hunger and thirst. That is their "foe" (verse 2).

What are the wanderers experiencing (verses 4-5)?

When they cry out to the LORD (verse 6), He hears them and does what for them (verses 7 and 9)?

The foe in this scenario is a combination of hunger, thirst, and no place to settle. The wanderers were hungry and thirsty. God provided their basic necessities of life and led them safely to a place where they could settle—a place they could call home. Isn't that a lovely word picture? These people were looking for a home, for purpose, and for satisfied hearts. God satisfied their needs.

We discussed what it means to be satisfied and unsatisfied in the Psalm 103 lesson. Let's look at what it means to have satisfied hearts.

Our God created us with a spiritual thirst for a relationship with Him (as the Bible declares). A relationship with another human cannot satisfy that thirst. Only God can satisfy the thirsty heart. His plan to do that included coming to earth to take on a human body and to live as a man among us. Enter Jesus.

Read Matthew 11:28-30.

What does Jesus invite you to do?

Jesus invites you to come to Him and find rest for your soul. You will no longer be a wanderer.

Women like security and that feeling of being settled. As the radical rabbi, Jesus treated women as no man had ever treated them before. His warmth, personal attention, tenderness, sound teaching, and compassion toward women were revolutionary. He openly demonstrated His love for each individual He met—both men and women—for whom He would ultimately die. A relationship with Jesus satisfies anyone's built-in spiritual thirst. Have you experienced that?

Those in Bondage

Focus on Psalm 107:10-16.

What are the people experiencing (verse 10)?

Why are they in bondage (verses 11-12)?

When they cry out to the LORD (verse 13), what does He do for them (verses 14 and 16)?

The foe in this scenario is bondage to something because of their rebellious hearts. This group had rebelled against the words of God and despised the counsel of God. To get their attention, He subjected them to bitter labor and helpless stumbling. In answer to their cries for help, God released them from their chains and brought them out of the darkness and gloom. He brought them into light. God can break down "gates of bronze" and "cut through bars of iron" (verse 16). Is any bondage too difficult for God to break? No!

God does the same for anyone who turns to Him in faith today.

Read Colossians 1:13-14.

God rescues you from what (verse 13, first part)?

And then He does what (verse 13, last part)?

The Bible says that every human is born into bondage to the slave master sin. It does not matter how much money and status we have nor our skin color and family history. We were born into bondage. We have a master and are a servant to something—either God and His righteousness or sin and its wickedness. There is no neutral ground. In that bondage, we are in spiritual darkness. And we have an enemy who does whatever he can to keep people in that darkness (2 Corinthians 4:4) so that we wander around looking for the light.

But God had compassion on all of us who were living in that dominion of darkness. He sent His Son to rescue us and bring us into His kingdom. There, we have redemption. There is that concept of being redeemed again. In Christ, we are set free from bondage to sin and rebellion. This has always been God's plan.

Once when Jesus was in His hometown of Nazareth, He was asked to speak in the local synagogue. In Luke 4, He read this from Isaiah 61:

> *"The Spirit of the Lord is on me, because he has anointed me to proclaim good news to the poor. He has sent me to **proclaim***

*freedom for the prisoners and recovery of sight for the blind, **to set the oppressed free**, to proclaim the year of the Lord's favor. … '**Today this scripture is fulfilled in your hearing**.'" (Luke 4:18-21)*

Jesus claimed to be the one fulfilling this function for people in spiritual bondage. He came to proclaim freedom for the prisoners and to set the oppressed free. Cutting through "bars of iron" (Psalm 107:16), He sets us free from our bondage to sin whenever we put our faith in Him. And He resettles us into His Kingdom.

Those Who Are Sick

Focus on Psalm 107:17-22.

What are the people experiencing and why (verses 17-18)?

When they cry out to the LORD (verse 19), what does He do for them (verse 20)?

How should they respond to His rescue (verse 22)?

The foe in this scenario is physical sickness and pain. They became fools through their rebellious ways and suffered affliction because of those sinful choices. They couldn't even eat and felt near death.

Most illness, pain, and physical disability are not caused by intentional sin but from living in a fallen world (Genesis 3). Some sickness and pain, however, are the consequences of intentional sin and can usually be recognized as such. Any healing we receive from any illness is still from God. We discussed this in the Psalm 103 lesson.

Notice how God's Word was part of their healing—*"He sent out his word and healed them; He rescued them from the grave."* This shows that spiritual nourishment can play a part in physical restoration of health. The gospels reference Jesus teaching people God's truth alongside His acts of healing (Matthew 4:23; 9:35; Mark 6:34).

Those in Sudden Peril

Focus on Psalm 107:23-32.

The foe in this scenario is trouble that comes upon us from no fault of our own. This would include natural disasters that God allows to happen.

Who are these people (verse 23)?

What are these merchants seeing as they sail on the seas (verse 24)?

Then what happened (verses 25-26)?

How did the danger affect them (verse 27)?

When they cry out to the LORD (verse 28), what does He do for them (verse 29-30)?

How should they respond to His rescue and restored security (verse 32)?

These verses describe people in business—merchants who are working hard to acquire and sell goods. Sailing the seas is required for their business. Getting onto a boat for each voyage brought risk to them—both their physical safety and financial security.

During their normal course of business on the seas, they saw the beauty of God's creation. The ocean can leave one feeling awestruck by its beauty and vastness. Many love the feel of the waves and seeing them roar onto a sandy beach. But a storm at sea can cause dangerously high waves that threaten to capsize any boat. That's what happened to this group of sailors causing their courage to melt (verse 26).

The NIV ends verse 27 with this phrase, "they were at their wits' end." That phrase came from the King James Version of the Bible (translated in 1611) and is now part of our everyday language.

If you have a business, have you ever been 'at your wits' end'? Did you cry out to God or freak out?

The merchants cried out to God to deliver them. He stilled the storm. Their hearts were glad when it grew calm. Then, they followed His direction to guide them to their desired haven. There, they used their social and economic platform to praise God and influence others to also praise Him.

God used such a storm at sea to change the life of a boat captain named John Newton in the mid-1700s. As a result, he wrote the song, "Amazing Grace" as a testimony to how God redeemed him. That is one of the best-known songs of praise to God worldwide.

Based upon Psalm 107, Jewish rabbis encouraged people to bring offerings of thanksgiving to God when anyone returned safely from a desert journey, release from prison or bondage, recovery from illness, and an ocean voyage.

Focus on Psalm 107:33-43.

The psalmist is looking back on all the good things that God does for His people as well as what He does to get the wicked, rebellious people to turn their hearts to Him. God can use any means to do that, including bringing what we call "natural disasters" (verses 33-34). He can also use His power to make wasteland into productive farmland (verse 35).

The writer is thinking about those he referenced in verses 4-9. What has God done for them (verses 36-38)?

Notice that they worked to provide. God multiplied their labor to satisfy their material needs. God feeds us through people. People design products and services to sell. They take the risk to start businesses and hire workers, including you. People plant crops and sell them to feed others.

Verses 39-40 may refer to the times when His people who were settled and doing well forgot about God and turned to wickedness again. We often see this in other places in the Old Testament.

When God shows His love to the needy (verse 41), how do the righteous and the wicked respond differently (verse 42)?

At the end of the psalm, the writer says to us, "Let the one who is wise heed these things and ponder the loving deeds of the Lord" (verse 43).

Why is it wise to heed the scenarios described here and ponder the loving deeds of the Lord?

Which of the four scenarios are similar to something you've experienced? How did the love of the Lord redeem you from similar troubles?

Look back and thank God; look forward and trust God. (anonymous quote on Facebook)

I love that my God is my redeemer. Do you love Him as your redeemer?

SONGS OF THE HEART

This whole psalm exalts the loyal love and mercy of our God. He has sovereign control of the forces of nature and can arrange circumstances in order to deliver us as we need it. This is a good psalm to read when we do not feel very thankful!

What do you learn about God from this psalm?

How does this psalm nourish your love for God?

Choose one verse from this psalm to write in the space below. Ask God to teach you through this verse.

You may have heard the song "Blessings" on the radio. Laura Story wrote words that fit very well with Psalm 107.

> We pray for blessings, We pray for peace
> Comfort for family, protection while we sleep
> We pray for healing, for prosperity
> We pray for Your mighty hand to ease our suffering
> And all the while, You hear each spoken need
> Yet love is way too much to give us lesser things
> 'Cause what if your blessings come through raindrops?
> What if Your healing comes through tears?
> What if a thousand sleepless nights
> Are what it takes to know You're near?
> What if my greatest disappointments, Or the aching of this life
> Is the revealing of a greater thirst, This world can't satisfy?
> And what if trials of this life, The rain, the storms, the hardest
> nights, are Your mercies in disguise?
>
> ("Blessings," song by Laura Story)

Pray: Thank God for His goodness to you and how He listens when you cry out to Him. Ask Him to help you praise Him publicly for His love and how He redeems you from bondage through your faith in Christ.

DEEPER DISCOVERIES (OPTIONAL):

Spend a few minutes reading and reflecting on the following psalms that speak of God's love for His people and how to show our gratitude to Him.

Read Psalm 27. Reflect on what you read.

Read Psalm 145. Reflect on what you read.

Psalm 139: My God Knows Me

Search me, God, and know my heart; test me and know my anxious thoughts. See if there is any offensive way in me, and lead me in the way everlasting. (Psalm 139:23-24)

Pray: Lord Jesus, please teach me through your Word.

Think about how you perceive yourself. Do you see yourself as valuable and precious with a voice and purpose? We looked at this somewhat in Psalm 8 (Lesson 1). You are specially created in the image of God.

> **If you struggle thinking of yourself as someone valuable to God with a purpose, what has influenced you otherwise?**

In this psalm, you will see how God wants you to think about yourself in light of what you know about Him.

PSALM 139

Like Psalm 34 (Lesson 34), this psalm written by David is a psalm of wisdom and praise. More than that, it is like a love letter from David to God—intensely personal. Read it with that in mind.

Read Psalm 139 silently then read it aloud.

> **In general, what is the writer feeling?**

> **What grabbed your attention from your reading?**

Did you notice the intimately personal relationship between God and humans? David used personal pronouns (me, my, I) more than 50 times. Yet, every 'I' and 'me' in this psalm applies not only to David but also to you (except maybe verses 19-22). Let's consider it that way.

Focus on Psalm 139:1-6.

Like Psalm 8, David opens and ends with similar wording (verses 1 and 23).

What can you know about God (verse 1)?

What does God know about you according to…

- Verse 2—

- Verse 3—

- Verse 4—

The fact that God knows everything (verse 4) is called His **omniscience**. God's omniscience can really baffle our minds! Notice how personal this is. David doesn't just say, "God knows all things." But he is basically saying, "God has known *me*." He emphasizes this three times. God knows you as well.

God knew David (and knows us) intimately because He wants to do so. The use of opposites (sit / rise and going out / lying down) represents completeness. David said that God was familiar with all his ways—

intimately acquainted. God knows your ways and thoughts, so He is not surprised by what you think, do, or say. He knows your needs before you even tell Him about them. He knows your strengths and weaknesses. He has no unrealistic expectations, nor can we deceive Him about our true selves.

We can't know God as much as He knows us. But as you have seen in this study, He wants us to know Him intimately. He reveals certain truths about Himself so that we may know Him better. We have seen those truths about God expressed in each of the psalms we have studied.

> *Can you hide anything from God? Does anything good or bad in your life escape His notice or surprise Him?*

> *How does it make you feel that God knows you so intimately? Are these thoughts comforting or frightening?*

Some may think this is intrusive. It all depends on your view of God—a loving Father who wants the best for you or a dictator ready to smite you whenever you do anything wrong. We looked at the truth in Psalm 103 (Lesson 5).

Notice how God knows these things about David's life but is not pulling strings like a puppeteer. God allows us free will to make choices. What could be the value of God knowing everything about you? Why would you even want this? Keep reading to find the answer to those questions.

> *David said that God's presence does what (verse 5)?*

To **hem in** means "to enclose, to encircle, to secure." This is evidence of God's protection as we saw in Psalm 34:7, *"The angel of the Lord encamps around those who fear him."* God protects you with His presence and power. His hand is upon you (Psalm 73:23). God is all-powerful. That is called His **omnipotence**.

God has our backs as He goes before us, behind us, and all around us. We all need that! God often uses people to do His work for Him. If you are surrounded by godly people whom God sends to surround you, that is in a sense being encircled by the hand of God.

David says that God's intimate knowledge of Him is what (verse 6)?

David's response is similar to what he wrote in Psalm 8. Awe! "Too wonderful for me." It is really beyond our comprehension. We cannot figure it out. Our response is to believe these truths so we can know about God's greatness and trust Him.

Focus on Psalm 139:7-12.

The writer asks what questions in verse 7?

Based on verse 8, what is the answer to those questions?

Even if you go far from home (verse 9), what is God still doing (verse 10)?

Why can't darkness hide you from God (verses 11-12)?

Again, you see the use of extremes (heights / depths and light / darkness) to represent completeness. The Old Testament writers spoke of *Sheol*, the place of the dead (verse 8), as though it were a huge underground cave where judgment takes place. Some translations use "the depths" rather than the word *Sheol*. It still represents the grave or realm of the dead.

The Bible teaches that God is everywhere at the same time. That is called His **omnipresence**. God is with you as you go about your daily schedule—to work, school, stores, or home. God is with you at each place. God is with you everywhere. In fact, wherever you go…He is already there!

God is not only there but His hand would be holding you close and guiding you (verse 10 and Psalm 73:23). Today, we have the presence of the Holy Spirit living inside us to guide and counsel us. He is forever with us.

You still have your freedom to choose and make decisions because God allows you to have that. Yet you are never out of His sight or reach. You cannot go to any place where God is not with you or cannot hear you calling out to Him. Even in the worst situation or location, you might not get a cell signal, but God is not blocked out! Ever!

These verses should give you hope if you have family members who have walked away from God. They can never escape from His presence regardless of where they are in this world. Darkness does not hide things from God's sight. In love, you can ask God to make life hard for them so they will cry out for His help as we saw in Psalm 107 (Lesson 6).

> You don't run away from God, my friend, even if you go to the moon! (J. Vernon McGee)

Neither can we escape God when we die (verse 8). There is existence after death. According to Philippians 2:10-11, everyone will one day bow down to Jesus—even those who are not permitted into heaven because they have rejected Him.

Can you go to a place where God is not with you or cannot hear you calling out to Him?

How does knowing God's omnipresence affect you?

When are some times that you need to remember that God is always wherever you are?

Focus on Psalm 139:13-18.

When did God begin to know you and how (verses 13 and 15)?

How are you to think about yourself in response to God's creating you (verse 14)?

How are you to think about those growing in their mothers' wombs?

What else does God know about you (verse 16)?

In Psalm 107:26, the writer used the phrase "the depths of the earth" for the grave. Here, David uses the same metaphor for the mother's womb along with "secret place." It is interesting how the two poets chose the same phrase to represent both the beginning and end of life.

David marveled at the Lord's amazing power in creating him from the moment of conception through fetal development and birth. These verses also confirm that having a physical human body is very good in God's eyes. When Jesus was resurrected from the dead, His new body was human. He is still in human form in heaven sitting at the right hand of God the Father.

The Lord's book (verse 16) is the book of the living. God determined David's length of life before he was even born. This could be the general human life span (70-80 years, Psalm 90:10) or specific for individuals. We die at all different ages with different causes of death. Whatever happens, God's plans for us are good.

God knows you well—having created you to be the special, unique person you are. He loves you dearly and knows you better than you know yourself. His plan and purpose for your life began while you were in your mother's womb.

From these verses (13-16), we have strong testimony to the fact that human life begins at conception rather than at birth.

What else is precious to David (verses 17-18)?

God's thoughts about us—how we are made, our ways, His protection—should be precious to us. We also have His thoughts in our Bibles. Do you consider His Word to be precious to you?

Thankfully, we can sleep while He handles the world. Yet, when we awake, He is still present with us. That is mind-blowing for sure!

Focus on Psalm 139:19-22.

David sees that God's adversaries do what (verse 20)?

What choice has David made (verse 21-22)?

The wicked are those who oppose God and are hostile to God's faithful ones (as in Psalm 73). We often see in David's writings his thoughts about the wicked who are not only David's adversaries but also God's. David looks around him, sees how much wickedness there is in the world, and sees how much trouble there is around him. He knows that God sees everything the wicked are doing and saying. He wants God to act in His justice (verse 19).

The word 'hate' as used in the psalms (verse 21) usually means rejection of someone or something. David recognizes the enemies of God, is offended by what they say and do, and chooses not to support them or be influenced by them. The choice David makes is staying loyal to God—that is, choosing to be aligned with people who are following God rather than fighting against Him. You can love enemies as God loves them but not let them win over you or those dear to you.

Focus on Psalm 139:23-24.

We have seen evidence of God's omniscience, omnipresence, and omnipotence in this psalm. You can know that those attributes of God are true about Him all the time. The amazing thing is that He chooses to use these powerful traits to take care of you!

As David said in Psalm 8:4, "What is mankind that you are mindful of them, human beings that you care for them?" You and I are significant to God. And we can trust the God who knows us.

David felt the same way. His response in concluding this psalm is a prayer straight from his heart.

> ***What does he ask God to keep doing to him and for him (verses 23-24)?***

David uses action verbs—search, test, see, and lead. David wanted God to test him, like a refiner tests ore to see if there is gold or silver in it. He wanted to stay loyal to God in his heart and life. Anxious thoughts are worries that indicate a lack of trust in God. Offensive ways would be any idolatrous tendencies taking David away from dependence on God to dependence on worldly things. David wants God to help him stay on a reliable path with God now and for future life with God forever.

Do you now see the value of God knowing everything about you? If you want the rewards of living life God's way, then you'll want help in recognizing when you are not doing it so you can change.

As David thinks about God knowing everything about him, he sees how much he **wants** God to know him fully—his heart, his thoughts, and his ways. God knows the truth about each of us as well, and He can reveal it to us for our benefit, as we allow Him to do so.

This is a good psalm to read whenever you feel that God has forsaken you. He has not!

> *Are you willing to give God permission to do the same in your life? What do you want Him to do?*

I love that my God knows me. Do you love that your God knows you and that you can know Him?

SONGS OF THE HEART

> *What do you learn about God from this psalm?*

> *How does this psalm nourish your love for God?*

> *Choose one verse from this psalm to write in the space below. Ask God to teach you through this verse.*

Use any creative means to express how God knows you so well and loves you dearly. A blank page is also included at the end of this lesson for you to use.

The song "Be Unto Your Name" was made popular by Robin Mark twenty years ago. It is still one of my favorites.

> We are a moment, You are forever
> Lord of the Ages, God before time
> We are a vapor, You are eternal
> Love everlasting, reigning on high
> We are the broken, You are the healer
> Jesus, Redeemer, Mighty to save
> You are the love song we'll sing forever
> Bowing before You, blessing Your name
> Holy, holy, Lord God Almighty
> Worthy is the Lamb Who was slain
> Highest praises, honor and glory
> Be unto Your name, be unto Your name
> ("Be unto Your Name," Gary Sadler and Lynn Deshazo)

Pray: Thank God for searching you so that He can know you well. Ask Him to help you appreciate His ever-presence with you and power He used to create your body. Ask Him to reveal your anxious thoughts so you can trust Him in those areas. Ask Him to lead you towards what is right and good in His eyes.

DEEPER DISCOVERIES (OPTIONAL):

Spend a few minutes reading and reflecting on the following psalms that speak of God's knowledge of you and love for you.

Read Psalm 100. Reflect on what you read.

Read Psalm 146. Reflect on what you read.

Hannah's Psalm—My Heart Trusts in My God

My heart rejoices in the LORD; in the LORD my horn is lifted high. My mouth boasts over my enemies, for I delight in your deliverance. (1 Samuel 2:1)

Pray: Lord Jesus, please teach me through your Word.

HISTORICAL INSIGHT

Time of the judges

Not long after Israel got settled in their land (recorded in the book of Joshua), the people began to adopt the religion and lifestyle of the pagans around them by worshipping idols and practicing immorality, theft, and murder. Because of their idolatry and hard hearts, God brought severe judgment on the land, allowing other nations to oppress and dominate His people for a time. This drove the people back to their God as they called to Him for help. God sent human leaders called "judges" to defeat the oppressing nations and bring periods of rest. Then, the land would experience peace for 20-40 years during the lifetime of the deliverer. Not long after that person died, the people went back to their wicked ways, beginning the cycle again. All of this is recorded in the book called "Judges."

The time of the judges covered ~325 years of Israel's history. Hannah lived in the last part of this time. Her son was the last judge of Israel before the kingdom began. So Hannah's story took place a few decades before David was born and began to write any of his psalms that we have studied.

Descriptive versus prescriptive

Much of the Old Testament is written in narrative form. That's what you find in the historical books (Genesis through Esther). Narrative means the text describes what happened. It is descriptive, not usually prescriptive. It is important to clarify the difference.

➢ **Descriptive** means the observation of what actually happened, how people lived, and choices they made at the time. For example, *"David and all the Israelites were celebrating with all their might before God, with songs and with harps, lyres, timbrels, cymbals and trumpets" (1 Chronicles 13:8)*. This is describing what they did. It is not a restriction on the types of instruments that can be used in worship.

➢ **Prescriptive** means a command from God about how to live or do something that applies to all believers, all people groups, and all time periods. For example, *"Give thanks to the Lord, for he is good; his love endures forever." (Psalm 107:1)*. This applies to every human who is alive or has ever lived.

Unless it is prescriptive, you can't take passages from Old Testament narratives and create a formula for doing things a certain way to guarantee God's blessing on the result. That is true in the case of Hannah and the vow that she made.

HANNAH'S STORY

Hannah, whose name means 'grace', was the beloved first wife of an Israelite man named Elkanah. But she was barren, so he married another woman. The 'sister wife' Peninah taunted Hannah and made her life miserable. Hannah had to endure this taunting for some time because Peninah had at least four children. Sadly, Elkanah did not understand Hannah's longing for a child.

One day when they were at one of the yearly festivals, Hannah went to the tabernacle and poured out her heart to God. Her story begins in utter helplessness.

Read 1 Samuel 1:9-28.

What did she ask from God and promise to do with His answer (verses 9-11)?

How did God answer her prayer (verses 17-20)?

Hannah was a godly woman. The Lord had closed her womb, yet she was not embittered against Him. Her husband was helpless to change her barrenness and passive in the destructive interaction between his wives. Hannah turned to the only one who could help her—God.

Praying "in deep anguish" and "weeping bitterly" before God graphically describes earnest, burdened prayer. Doing so releases anxiety and leads one to submit to God and trust in Him as we have seen in Psalm 34 and Psalm 107. God enables us to feel peace in our problem as He did for Hannah (1 Samuel 1:18).

God remembered Hannah (1 Samuel 1:19). To 'remember' in the Bible is not merely to recall to mind. It is to express concern for someone and to act with loving care on their behalf. God did that.

Hannah promised her son for a lifetime of service to God, similar to wanting your children to dedicate themselves to serve God. Hannah gave her child to God to serve Him as a godly leader for Israel. Samuel's name means "God hears." He does! We saw that clearly declared in Psalm 34 and Psalm 107. God blessed Hannah with fertility—Samuel plus several more children—and blessed Israel with a spiritual leader.

When Samuel was 3-4 years old, Hannah fulfilled her vow to God. When she brought Samuel to live at the Tabernacle to serve Him, what did she say (verses 27-28)?

As I mentioned earlier, this is a descriptive narrative not a prescription for how one should pray for or parent children.

Such voluntary vows were common in Old Testament times. They were regulated by the law (Numbers 30) and were expected to be carefully thought out (Proverbs 20:25). Once the vow was fulfilled, the worshipper would bring offerings of thanks to God at the Tabernacle or later to the Temple.

Vows other than marriage vows are not generally taught or modeled in the New Testament. Nowhere are Gentiles encouraged to make vows other than faithfulness to God with their lives.

HANNAH'S PRAYER PSALM

Once she fulfilled the vow she made to God, Hannah prayed a psalm that was then recorded in the Bible for us to know.

Read 1 Samuel 2:1-10 silently then read it aloud.

In general, what is Hannah feeling?

What grabbed your attention from your reading?

Focus on 1 Samuel 2:1-2.

Her heart is doing what (verse 1)?

In what does she delight (verse 1)?

What does she think about God (verse 2)?

Like the other psalms we have studied, Hannah's song is a poem that uses symbolism to illustrate her thoughts. The term "horn" (verses 1 and 10) is frequently used in the Old Testament to symbolize strength.

Focus on 1 Samuel 2:3.

Why should someone not keep talking proudly?

Between verses 1 and 3, Hannah contrasts boasting in the Lord versus boasting in one's own life with arrogance. That is a continual theme in the Bible. God will humble people who view themselves as self-sufficient. As you learned in Psalm 139, our God is one who knows everything. He sees everything. He knows what people are doing and saying. Their "deeds are weighed" (judged).

Focus on 1 Samuel 2:4-5.

Continuing her knowledge about God, Hannah mentions three contrasts here regarding situations in which someone can boast.

Why should someone not boast in their own situation?

What can God do for the one who stumbles, is hungry, or barren?

At any time, the good situations can be taken away. Yet God will help those who cast themselves on Him. They will be strengthened and have their needs satisfied.

Focus on 1 Samuel 2:6-10.

What does Hannah know to be true about God in these verses...

- Verse 6—

- Verse 7—

- Verse 8—

- Verse 9—

- Verse 10—

Hannah's prayer is her psalm of praise and thanksgiving. She expresses her emotions and still affirms truths about God that she knows—His holiness and power (verse 2), wisdom and justice (verse 3), and sovereignty (verses 6-10). She has been taught well.

Hannah's prayer song is also prophetic, anticipating the establishment of kingship in Israel (verse 10). Her son Samuel crowns the first king, Saul, as well as the second king, David. In verse 10, her song contains the first reference in the Bible to the Lord's anointed. "Anointed" is the Hebrew word *mashiyach* from which 'Messiah' is derived. The Greek translation of this Hebrew term is 'Christos', from which comes the English word 'Christ'.

Did you notice that this prayer contains no petition? But it definitely articulates Hannah's belief that God rewards trust with blessing. Hannah believes and expresses that people should trust in the Lord. God will bless those who want to further His purposes in the world by making it possible for them to do that. Natural limitations do not limit God.

More than 1000 years later, another woman sang a psalm to God. She also was taught well and likely knew Hannah's song.

Read Luke 1:46-55.

After Mary received the announcement from the angel Gabriel that she would soon be pregnant with Jesus, she hurriedly left Nazareth and traveled 70 miles to visit her relative Elizabeth. Elizabeth confirmed to Mary that she was indeed carrying the promised Messiah. Mary spontaneously burst out in her own psalm. Mary's praise song is similar to Hannah's song.

Like Hannah, Mary's heart is doing what (verses 46-47)?

Why (verses 48-49)?

What does Mary know about God (verses 50-51)?

Mary's song reflects her knowledge of God and His Word, including the psalms that we have studied. You can also see similarities to Hannah's song—the holiness of God and how He exalts those who are humble and humbles those who are arrogant (verses 52-53).

Our God understands women. As Creator, He designed us with a mind to know God, emotions to love God, and a will to obey God. Our female minds should be filled with the knowledge of Him so that our hearts may respond with great love for Him, and our wills can choose to obey Him.

Hannah and Mary demonstrate those truths in their lives. They chose to fill their minds with the knowledge of God. Their hearts responded with love for Him. And their wills chose to obey Him. May we do likewise!

God and prayer

As we have seen in this study of Psalms, God uses prayer to get us into partnership with Him. In His presence, we more likely to recognize His blessings to us. And we should not think we have to go to a special place in order to pray to God. Hannah went to the tabernacle. But we have seen that David poured out his heart anytime, anywhere. God heard him from wherever he was. He does the same for us.

Read Hebrews 4:14-16.

Who is helping us as we pray and how?

Read Romans 8:26-27

Who is helping us as we pray?

Read Romans 8:31-34.

Who is helping us as we pray?

To intercede means to act on our behalf. Jesus is the mediator of our salvation because of our faith in Him. He also acts on our behalf as does God the Father and God the Spirit. All work together to answer our needs and satisfy our hearts.

How does knowing this make you feel?

I love that my heart can trust in my God. Does your heart trust in God as well?

SONGS OF THE HEART

What do you learn about God from Hannah's story and psalm?

How does Hannah's psalm nourish your love for God?

Choose one verse from Hannah's psalm to write in the space below. Ask God to teach you through this verse.

Hannah needed God. So do we. The modern psalm, "Lord, I Need You," is one of my favorite reminders of how much we need our trustworthy Lord's help every single day of our lives.

Lord I come, I confess, Bowing here, I find my rest
Without You, I fall apart, You're the one that guides my heart
Where sin runs deep, Your grace is more
Where grace is found is where You are
And where You are, Lord, I am free, Holiness is Christ in me
Lord, I need You, oh, I need You, Every hour, I need You
My one defense, my righteousness, Oh God, how I need You
So teach my song to rise to You
When temptation comes my way
And when I cannot stand, I'll fall on You
Jesus, You're my hope and stay
Lord, I need You, oh, I need You, Every hour, I need You
My one defense, my righteousness, Oh God, how I need You
("Lord, I Need You," Matt Maher)

DEEPER DISCOVERIES (OPTIONAL):

Spend a few minutes reading and reflecting on the following psalms that speak of God's holiness and greatness.

Read Deborah's song in Judges 5:1-31. Reflect on what you read.

Read Psalm 46. Reflect on what you read.

Note: The phrase "according to *alamoth*" is a musical term meaning that it was to be sung by the voices of young women. We know that the temple choir included both male and female singers (1 Chronicles 25:5-6; Nehemiah 7:67).

Sources

The following resources were used in the preparation and writing of this study.

1. *A Woman After God's Own Heart,* Crossroads Bible Church Women's Ministry 2000.
2. Bob Deffinbaugh, "What is a Psalm?" Bible.org.
3. *Dr. Tom Constable's Notes on Psalms 2024 Edition.*
4. Ian Thomas, *The Saving Life of Christ.*
5. J. Vernon McGee, *Thru the Bible with J. Vernon McGee.* Volume 2.
6. John F. Walvoord and Roy B. Zuck, *The Bible Knowledge Commentary Old Testament*, Victor Books, 1985.
7. Kris Murphy, *God Reveals, We Respond.*
8. Stanley Toussaint, "God's Revelation and Our Response," Dallas Theological Seminary.
9. Sue Edwards, *Psalms.*
10. *The NIV Study Bible New International Version,* Zondervan Bible Publishers, 1985.
11. Wayne Braudrick, "Sermon on Psalm 46," 1/5/25.

Songs at the end of each lesson

Lesson 1: "The Majesty and Glory of Your Name," Linda Lee Johnson and Tom Fettk

Lesson 2: "Sing the Mighty Power of God," Isaac Watts

Lesson 3: "Whom Shall I Fear," Chris Tomlin, Ed Cash, Scott Cash

Lesson 4: "Blessed Be Your Name," Matt Redman, Beth Redman

Lesson 5: "Who Am I?" Mark Hall

Lesson 6: "Blessings," Laura Story

Lesson 7: "Be unto Your Name," Gary Sadler and Lynn Deshazo

Lesson 8: "Lord, I Need You," Matt Maher